Pizza Quest

Also by Peter Reinhart

Perfect Pan Pizza

Peter Reinhart's Whole Grain Breads

Bread Revolution

Peter Reinhart's Artisan Breads Every Day

American Pie: My Search for the Perfect Pizza

The Joy of Gluten-Free, Sugar-Free Baking
(with Denene Wallace)

Crust and Crumb

The Bread Baker's Apprentice

Brother Juniper's Bread Book

Sacramental Magic in a Small-town Café

Bread Upon the Waters

Pizza Quest

My Never-Ending Search for the Perfect Pizza

Peter Reinhart

Andrews McMeel
PUBLISHING®

Pizza Quest

Andrews McMeel Publishing
a division of Andrews McMeel Universal
1130 Walnut Street, Kansas City, Missouri 64106

www.andrewsmcmeel.com

22 23 24 25 26 SHO 10 9 8 7 6 5 4 3 2 1

ISBN: 978-1-5248-6700-3

Library of Congress Control Number: 2021948673

Editor: Allison Adler
Art Director: Holly Swayne
Production Editor: Meg Daniels
Production Manager: Carol Coe

Attention: Schools and Businesses

Andrews McMeel books are available at quantity discounts with bulk purchase
for educational, business, or sales promotional use. For information, please e-mail
the Andrews McMeel Publishing Special Sales Department:
specialsales@amuniversal.com.

Contents

The Pizzas . . . 45

Round Pies . . . 47

Square and Other Pan Pizzas . . . 105

Focaccia, Roman, Stuffed, and Specialty Pies 131

Introduction

Pizza Quest the book was born out of *Pizza Quest* the web series, which was born out of my first book, *American Pie: My Search for the Perfect Pizza,* written *way* back in 2003. In other words, this "quest," and my life as a self-described "pizza freak," has been going on publicly for a while but, really, for my whole life—with no end of questing in sight.

A few years after the publication of *American Pie,* I was approached by two kindred spirits, fellow pizza freaks from Los Angeles, Brad English and Jeff Michael, who happened to also be commercial television producers. They proposed the idea of continuing my story where *American Pie* left off, but this time as a television series. We were able to put together enough financial backing, with a lot of pro bono help from their friends in the business, and filmed a road trip up the California coast from Los Angeles to San Francisco with visits to some amazing pizzerias and artisan food producers, which eventually became the first season of what Brad and Jeff titled *Pizza Quest.*

We launched the series with sponsorship from Forno Bravo Wood-Fired Ovens, with additional support from BelGioioso Cheese, Central Milling, Bianco DiNapoli, and Fire Within. All the money we raised went into production costs and editing our raw footage into short webisodes. It became our pilot season and, eventually, got us a season on a new network launched by Craftsy called Bluprint (owned at the time by NBC). Meanwhile, I kept writing books on bread while our pizza questing led me to all sorts of relationships and opportunities in the pizza world. I judged at a few competitions and witnessed the dynamic growth of the pan pizza category, which included Roman–style, Detroit– style, and a number of wonderful "square" types of pizza, inspiring me to write a book called *Perfect Pan Pizza,* published in 2019, to explore that phenomenon. I also began speaking at the annual International Pizza Expo in Las Vegas and at other pizza conferences, and when we could, Brad, Jeff, and I kept filming new episodes of *Pizza Quest* to post on our site.

And then the COVID-19 pandemic hit.

The restaurant community, like everyone else, was devastated, and an early casualty was the 2020 International Pizza Expo, leaving its 10,000 attendees bereft and jonesing for that soul-satisfying, yearly tribal connection to which we had all become accustomed. Noel Brohner (featured here on page 74) gathered a few of his tech-savvy friends and figured out how to create a virtual Zoom pizza party, and many of the scheduled speakers and attendees from the Expo signed on. For four days we all gathered on-screen—during the exact days when the Expo was supposed to be happening—to commiserate and lament, but also to celebrate our fellowship. It was my first inkling of how the world as I knew it had changed and merged with the digital world, and it gave me an idea.

I met with Brad and Jeff, and we designed a Zoom interview show where I could dive deeper, on a one-on-one basis, with many of the pizza luminaries I'd come to know via the Expo and our various *Pizza Quest* travels. We started recording these interviews and posting them on our website, as well as across various social media platforms. By the end of the summer, we had recorded over 100 hours, and *Pizza Talk* was off and running.

After we had been on the air for a few months, we met with the folks at Heritage Radio Network (HRN), a podcast network dedicated to food-themed content, and they agreed to repurpose the video interviews into audio podcasts. Before long we were able to reach even more listeners. Hey, the "pizza-freak nation" is vast, and it's extremely passionate.

The most exciting outcome of *Pizza Talk,* for me, is that the guests who appeared—some of the greatest pizza makers in the world—who represented an unlimited storehouse of creativity and pizza recipes that many people would never experience unless they happened to be in the same city as their pizzerias. I proposed an idea, first to my wonderful publisher, Kirsty Melville of Andrews McMeel, and, once she was enthused, then to the many guests who had appeared on *Pizza Talk.* Here's what my proposal was:

> *How about a book that features recipes based on the spectacular, award-winning pizzas of my guests, but without giving away any secrets or requiring the reader to follow the exact dough formulas and specialty ingredient sourcing that these pizza geniuses have spent years developing? I'll call their original versions the "hero pizzas," and the pizzaiolos will provide just enough ingredient and assembly information for me to "cover" their recipes in this book. In other words, these will be like very good covers of the greatest hits of the pizza geniuses. If they are the Beatles, then I'll be the Beatles tribute band.*

That was my pitch, and lo and behold, the pizzaiolos all joined in, and as you will see in the pages that follow, the hits are great indeed!

Of course, these amazing pizzas represent only a small fraction of the greatness that lies out there in the pizza world, and the artists featured in this book are by no means the only ones worthy of being represented here. They just happen to be the ones I know and love and who were willing to contribute to this book. I've merely scratched the surface of the talent that exists in the pizza community. Even as I write these words, we continue recording new interviews with those who didn't appear during our first season, so who knows? If you like this book, there's no end of talent and perfect pizzas still to cover as my never-ending quest continues.

My goal here is to show you, using my own experience as a serious dough guy and lifelong pizza freak, how to make pizzas like these Beatles-level originals—or at least get you into the same concert hall with them so you can create your own cover versions. For those of you already in the pizza business, there could be some useful tips and tricks and menu ideas here, but more importantly, even home cooks want to know what the experts know, or, to keep playing with these metaphors, we all want to play in Fenway Park (or Wrigley Field, or Yankee Stadium—you get my point), so this is my playbook for how you can get into the game.

My method is simple: I have provided you with four master dough formulas, with a number of variations to use when appropriate, that will enable you to make tribute versions of all the pizzas in this book. You will also find an all-purpose crushed tomato sauce that's my go-to—not the same ones as the "hero" recipe originators use, but my own—as well as my so-called "secret" hoagie sauce, which you can use on just about anything and, for sure, on many of these pizzas (being originally from Philly,

I am required to be a huge fan of hoagies and hoagie sauces). Finally, based on what each of these featured pizza geniuses told me, I'll provide you with the recipe and steps to make your own tribute pizza, based on my tribute pizza, based on their hero, gold-standard versions.

You'll also see photos of the pizzas—beauty shots—provided by the originators themselves, so you'll know what your target is. I found these shots really helpful and inspirational as I developed my cover versions, and so will you. In addition, we shot a number of instructional photos illustrating the techniques for mixing, shaping, and panning your pizzas that will prove helpful for newbies and veterans alike. Throughout, I provide commentary for each recipe and a little background on each of our pizza luminaries, and I encourage you to look them on up online or follow them on social media if you want to drill deeper into their individual repertoires.

As you can see, I love metaphors as much as I love pizza, and the tradition of the "quest" is one of the most ancient and powerful of images. But I believe in such quests, and I also believe the secret to life is to recognize that we are each on our own quest for deeper meaning and purpose. For me, bread and pizza have served as useful symbols—icons, actually—that are like windows into the mind of our Creator. Anything we love can serve as such an icon, leading us in search of joy and fulfillment. Who would have thought that pizza could be such a window? But it is—and not just for me, as I've learned during my quest. In fact, one of the most important things I've learned during these years in search of the perfect pizza is that it is more about the quest than it is about the pizza—and the quest never ends.

The Ten Commandments of *Pizza Quest*

Every quest needs a creed and a guidebook. Just as the Ten Commandments serve in that capacity for my faith tradition, the following commandments are the key takeaways and nuggets of wisdom I've discovered during my pizza journey. Unlike the original Ten Commandments, these are not set in stone and are subject to change, but I share them with you in the hope that you might draw up your own quest guidebook. Until then, though, feel free to use mine:

1. There are only two kinds of pizza: good and very good. And by very good, I mean great, and by great, I mean memorable—memorableness means you can't stop thinking about it, can't wait to go back, can't wait to take your friends. This is the determination of greatness.
2. There is no such thing as the perfect pizza; there are only perfect pizzas. (Thank you, Howard Moskowitz and Malcolm Gladwell, for this concept).
3. When it comes to toppings, more is not always better; better is better.
4. Great pizza always starts with a great crust. An average crust with great toppings can never be more than interesting, while a great crust with barely any toppings can still be a great pizza.
5. Respect the craft. (Thank you, Tony Gemignani, for coining that phrase and printing it on every box.)
6. The single most important tools for pizza makers are our hands; "these hands" are the mark of a true artisan. (Thank you, Rob DiNapoli and John Arena, for coining that phrase and starting the These Hands movement.)
7. When it comes to bread or pizza dough, understanding fermentation is the key, and time is the most important ingredient.
8. A recipe is a template, a guideline, but it is not a law. Understand the letter, but follow the spirit.
9. The only pizza rule that matters is the "flavor rule"; that is, flavor rules!
10. Tradition should be honored and respected, but as a verb, not a noun. Pizza tradition is constantly expressing itself anew in the ever-present now.

Getting Started

If you're planning to make pizzas from this book, I would guess this is not your first pizza rodeo. However, those brave enough to dive in without as much experience may need some guidance as to how to get organized. Most of the instructions are built into each of the recipes, but there will be the assumption that you are in possession of the basic tool kit. I'm not talking about elaborate or hard-to-find equipment, just your basic pizza mise en place. (Note: These recipes are designed for home ovens, not wood-fired brick ovens or even the new generation of portable brick ovens. You can use those but will have to adjust the temperatures for each pizza. But if you already have one of those, you're probably far enough along to not need much advice from me on how to use them.)

The following list is for those of you who are relatively new to making pizzas at home. Here's what you'll need:

- **A baking stone or baking steel** that fits in your oven and covers most, but not all, of your oven rack. Baking steels, which are relatively new tools, are indestructible and fabulous conductors of heat but more expensive and heavier than baking stones. There is a lot of info on the internet about them, and we did an extensive interview with Andris Lagsdin, inventor of the original baking steel, on *Pizza Talk,* if you want to learn more.

  Baking stones, on the other hand, come in varying shapes and degrees of thickness. Generally, the thicker the better, and rectangular is better than round, but any stone is better than no stone. As you get more experience, you may even want to have two stones for double-rack baking. Always allow about an hour for these thermal masses to absorb the oven heat before baking on them.

- **A digital kitchen scale,** preferably one that measures in both pounds/ounces and grams. There are many brands available at a reasonable cost (under fifty dollars and as low as twenty-five dollars). In some recipes, I give measurements in both weight and volume/spoon measurements, especially for items that are so light as to be easier to measure by teaspoons or tablespoons. However, for flour, water, and many topping ingredients, weights are always more reliable. And for flour and water, I highly advise not measuring by volume, as a cup of flour or water will vary from person to person depending on how one scoops the flour or eyeballs the water, but ounces or grams will be the same for all of us.

- **A cheese grater,** preferably a box-style grater with four sides of various holes and slits. You can also use a food processor with grating and shredding attachments.

- **A roller-style pizza knife** or, for those who plan to make a lot of pizzas, a **curved mezzaluna-style rocker knife.** If you have neither, a good chef's knife will do.

- **A good set of sharp knives,** both large and small.

- **12 by 18-inch sheet pans (1 inch tall),** as well as **round or rectangular cake or brownie pans or, even better, Detroit–style pizza pans** (available online), which are typically **2¼ inches tall** and come in various dimensions. I suggest 6 by 6-inch pans for small pizzas, 8 by 10-inch pans for medium size, and 10 by 14-inch pans for family size. Many of the baking pans you may already possess could also work, so follow the chart on page 12 for instructions on how much dough and cheese is appropriate for each size pan. Also, round cake pans can be used in place of square or rectangular pans, as long as they are more than 2 inches high.

- **Sturdy cutting boards.**
- **Baking parchment that can be cut to fit, or silicone baking pads (such as Silpats)** designed to fit 12 by 18-inch sheet pans.
- **Plastic bowl scrapers, metal bench blades, and various sizes of plastic and metal spatulas and flippers.**
- **Heavy-duty pot holders.** These pans get very hot (enough said).
- **Saucepans and whisks.**
- **An electric dough mixer** (optional, as these doughs can also be mixed by hand in a bowl).
- **A pizza peel, either wooden or metal.** One of each type is even better, since the wooden peels are easier to use for loading the pizzas, and the thinner metal peels are better for retrieving them from the oven.

That's about it. And if you find yourself missing a tool you think you need, do what the rest of us often do: improvise.

FAQ

Can I swap out different cheeses for the ones listed?

Yes, many cheeses will work in these recipes, but some are better for melting, and others, especially aged, dry cheeses such as Parmesan and Romano, provide wonderfully intense flavor but no "cheese pull." When substituting some of your favorite cheeses for the ones listed, stay in the same family or style of cheese, such as Gouda or Muenster for fontina, and the like. As usual, the only rule that matters here is the "flavor rule" (that is, flavor rules!), so feel free to swap in your favorites as long as they taste good and serve the overall balance of flavors.

Can I use a different dough than the one listed for the recipe?

If you already have a favorite dough recipe you think will work for the pizza listed, of course, go for it. My versions are tributes to the originals, and yours can be, too. You can also mix and match the dough recipes, using any given one on a pizza that calls for another. There are an unlimited number of permutations, and the goal here is to unlock your own creativity so you can design great pizzas to your own liking.

Can I modify a dough recipe by adding whole-grain or specialty flour?

Yes. Some of the pizzas in this book call for slight flour adjustments or swap-ins, but you are always free to swap in specialty flours of your choice, even when not called for in the recipe. However, if you are adding in whole-grain flour to replace some of the white flour, increase the water slightly—usually ½ ounce (14 grams) of water for every 2 ounces (57 grams) of whole-grain flour.

What about salt substitutions and types?

Most of the recipes call for either kosher salt or coarse or flake sea salt. All are, in reality, variations of sea salt, though some salts contain a small amount of minerals as well. The real difference, though, is how much they weigh. Fine salt is denser than coarse or kosher salt because there's more air in a spoonful of kosher, flake, or coarse salt than in a spoonful of finely ground salt, such as table salt. I like to reserve flake salt for use as a finishing seasoning added after the pizza comes out of the oven, since a little goes a long way and it doesn't immediately dissolve into the ingredients but, instead, provides a nice salty flavor burst. Otherwise, as long as you weigh the salt rather than use teaspoons and tablespoons, you are guaranteed to use the correct amount.

Convection vs. conventional/radiant ovens

Every oven is unique, and even convection ovens bake differently from one another depending on the brand. Typically, a low convection setting will allow you to bake at 25°F lower than in a conventional oven, or 50°F lower if using a strong convection. I like convection ovens for pizzas baked on a stone, baking steel, or other thick, solid baking surface, because the heat is more efficiently distributed, and you can usually complete the bake a minute or two sooner with convection, which results in a crisper crust while maintaining a moist, creamy interior. But when baking Detroit, Roman, Sicilian, and other "square" pies, I prefer conventional baking, because you can get more bottom heat, allowing the under-crust to get crisp before the cheese melts and over-browns. Again, there are exceptions to this guideline, and in the end, your particular oven will dictate how to best set it and on which rack to bake your pizza.

What is cupping pepperoni?

Pepperoni, already the most popular of all toppings, is having an artisan moment, with many charcuterie, salumeria, and specialty sausage companies getting into the game. Even the major producers have come out with a cherished style, at a reasonable price, designed to curl into a cup-like, crisp disc on the pizza. This new generation of pepperoni is one of those phenomena that develops its own cult-like following and is a win-win for all of us pepperoni lovers.

Can I use bacon fat, lard, or even shortening to grease my pans?

Yes, bacon fat almost always makes things taste better—and chicken schmaltz (page 77) is equally functional. However, my usual method is either olive oil or a blend of olive oil and melted butter. An advantage of using a solid fat for greasing a pan pizza is that it helps hold the dough in place as it cools, and butter, of course, tastes better than shortening or even lard. But bacon fat—whoa!—that's on a whole different level, so feel free to use it if you have it ("smoke 'em if you got 'em," as the saying goes).

Pluses and minuses of prebaking the crust

Some of these recipes instruct you to prebake the crust and add the toppings later for the re-bake. Others are designed for one long, single bake. In many instances, the processes are interchangeable, as I learned from the great Detroit–style pizza masters Shawn Randazzo and Jeff Smokevitch. In the past, Detroit–style pizzas were always done in one bake, but after they surged in popularity, it became necessary to use the re-bake method to keep up with the orders. My early attempts at re-baking produced crusts that seemed drier and less creamy or moist and custard-like in the crumb. But with practice came success, and many of the popular square pizza places are now almost exclusively doing prebake/re-bake because it allows them to get the pizzas out much faster. There's a risk of overbaking the crust and drying it out with this method, but if you follow the guidelines in this book, you shouldn't have that problem.

What rack in the oven should I use?

Every oven bakes differently, so I suggest starting out on the middle rack (or the lower middle if your oven doesn't have a center middle rack). After a few bakes, you'll be able to ascertain whether to bake on a lower rack (or a higher one) based on how your oven performs, resulting in both the under-crust and the topping side finishing at the same time, with a golden underside and bubbly, caramelized cheese on top. Also, if baking on more than one rack, it's important to rotate and switch the pans onto different shelves during the bake so all pans get exposed to the direct bottom heat.

What if I can't find Mike's Hot Honey?

Many pizzerias have discovered Mike's Hot Honey during the past few years, and it has really been a game-changer. Mike was brilliant in marrying cayenne with honey and very smart to use a proprietary type of cayenne pepper. His honey is beginning to find itself on retail shelves, but it's still mainly a food service product, so if you can't find it, you can make your own by whisking cayenne pepper into your favorite local honey. How much? That really depends on you and your audience, but remember that a little goes a long way. Start with ½ teaspoon of cayenne in 1 cup of honey, then add more if you think it needs it. Will it be as good as Mike's? Well, all I know is that he spent a lot of time finding a particular pepper and testing the proportions to make his version perfect. As with this whole book, consider your own homemade hot honey a tribute version of Mike's.

How do I make the butter paste for greasing the pans for Detroit–style or square pizzas?

There's no one right way for this—after all, you can accomplish the same greasing with just olive or vegetable oil. But I like the solid fat function of butter and also the flavor when mixed with olive oil. I use 2 parts olive oil to 1 part butter most of the time but have been known to go 50-50. No rules govern this. However, I suggest using softened butter or, if melting, do it slowly and pull it off the heat as soon as it melts rather than letting it brown.

What if my pans are a different size than the ones called for in the recipes?

Use the chart below for dough and cheese amounts per pan size. If your pan doesn't show up on the chart, calculate the square inches (width times length), then find a pan close in size and use that number. Detroit–style pizzas are typically baked in square or rectangular steel or aluminum pans, with sidewalls of about 2¼ inches tall (or more). But they can also be baked in round pans, such as cake pans, as long as the side walls are more than 2 inches tall. While the recipes in this book indicate suggested pan dimensions, rather than ordering new pans, you are also free to use other size pans that you may have on hand, by following this chart for both dough and cheese weight. Remember, these weights are guidelines, but you are free to tweak these amounts to your own taste.

Pan Size	Dough Weight	Total Cheese Weight
6" X 6"	5 ounces / 142 g	4 ounces / 113 g
8" X 8"	8 ounces / 227 g	6 ounces / 170 g
9" X 9"	10 ounces / 284 g	7.5 ounces / 213 g
9" X 13"	14 ounces / 397 g	10 ounces / 284 g
8" X 10"	10 ounces / 284 g	7.5 ounces / 213 g
10" X 14"	16 ounces / 454 g	12 ounces / 340 g
6" round	4 ounces / 113 g	3 ounces / 85 g
8" round	6.5 ounces / 184 g	4.5 ounces / 128 g
9" round	8 ounces / 227 g	6 ounces / 170 g
10" round	9.5 ounces / 269 g	7.5 ounces / 213 g

How do I make the cheese around the perimeter of the pan form a crispy "crown"?

A number of the pizza geniuses in this book like to use grated cheddar cheese for the crown effect, where the cheese forms a lacy, crispy fringe around the perimeter, above the crust. Cheddar also works nicely for the crispy *frico* on the outside walls of the crust. Some pizza makers even spread the grated cheddar or other cheese on a pan and dry it out slightly, overnight in the fridge, to promote a lacy, crown-like effect. Brick cheese will also work, as will provolone and Gouda, but white cheddar (mild or medium aged is fine) seems to be the consensus champ. Do not use dry aged cheeses such as Parmesan or Romano other than to line the inside walls of the pan; if they sit unprotected on top of the crust, they're likely to burn before the crust is finished baking. You can, however, mix in a little grated aged cheese (about 25% of the total blend) with your moister cheeses to promote the lacing/crowning effect.

If a recipe calls for Romano, can I substitute Parmesan, or vice versa?

Some people are more sticklers about this than I am, as I find all types of dry aged cheeses to be equally delicious and interchangeable, subject to your personal preference and allegiance to specific cheese regions. Whether you choose true Parmigiano-Reggiano or domestic knockoffs, dry Jack, Asiago, Grana Padano (a variant of Parmesan), or Pecorino Romano (made from goat's or sheep's milk), when you're using them as a garnishing cheese, you should use the one you like to eat; when baking with it as part of a cheese blend, most of the subtle nuances are obscured by the melting and the other ingredients. There really is no wrong choice when garnishing with any of these cheeses, so use what you have and what you like. Once again, the "flavor rule" applies.

What's the difference between grated and shredded cheese?

I use these terms throughout the book. Shredded refers to grating the cheese on the larger grater holes to make longer strands, and is usually reserved for moister, meltier cheeses. Grated cheese refers to cheese grated through the smaller holes or slits for a finer, almost powdery result, and is more appropriate for dry aged cheeses, especially when using them as a finishing garnish.

Can I still make the Neapolitan pizzas if I don't have a baking stone or a baking steel?

Yes. This is a better-than-nothing hack: Invert a 12 by 18-inch sheet pan and use the underside of the pan as your baking platform. While it won't absorb the same amount of heat as the more solid thermal masses, such as a stone or a baking steel, it will work in a pinch. And, as the saying goes, any pizza is better than no pizza.

How can I combine sourdough starter and commercial instant yeast for a "spiked," or mixed, method?

You can always "spike" your pizza dough with a small amount of instant yeast. Many pizzerias do this, as it provides a safety net of reliability to the rise and also shortens the fermentation time, making a less sour-tasting dough compared with a pure sourdough. This is sometimes called the "mixed method of fermentation." In the sourdough recipe in this book, I list an optional amount of instant yeast "spike" equal to 0.5 percent of the total flour weight. This is consistent with the amount of yeast used in the non-sour pizza doughs. You do, however, have the option of reducing the amount of yeast in your "spike." Some pizzerias drop this down to 0.25 percent of yeast to flour, which still speeds the fermentation somewhat but also allows more time for flavor development. Some versions even drop that percentage down to 0.1 percent, which slows the fermentation time significantly but is still faster than using dough leavened by only the starter. In other words, you're free to play with these ratios. If you use the full 0.50 percent ratio, your sourdough starter serves more as a pre-ferment than as the primary leavening agent, but still adds considerable complexity and flavor to the dough. This is ideal if you want the reliable time frame of a standard pizza dough while retaining some of the tang and depth of flavor that sourdough provides. As you play with these ratios, you'll soon find the "sweet spot" that works best for you in the balancing act between time and flavor development.

What is flour strength, and which flours are appropriate for particular pizzas?

There are many opinions about what types and strengths of flour are best for pizza dough. The short answer is (as so often is the case) that it depends. Personal preference is as much a factor as historical authenticity, but it helps to know the functionalities of different types of flours to help you choose.

The master dough recipes in this book call mainly for bread flour (unbleached if possible) because it's what I like for texture and flavor. Others may disagree and prefer to use all-purpose or Italian-style 00 flour, or even high-gluten flour. So here are a few of the differences: White flour made from wheat can be considered either soft or hard, which refers to the percentage of protein—primarily gluten protein—the flour produces. Anything under 10 percent is considered soft, between 10 and 11.5 percent is all-purpose, between 11.5 and 13 percent is bread flour, and above 13 percent is considered high-gluten flour. Other countries have different ways of categorizing their flour, but this is the predominant American system.

High-gluten flour is typically used in New York–style slice pizzas and also in pizza dough with additional flour types, such as whole wheat or other grains. High-gluten flour, when used for pizza dough, typically also includes a fair amount of fat or oil to help counteract the hardness of the wheat—sometimes as much as 8 to 10 percent oil to flour. Protein is what makes flour hard, so the higher the protein, the harder the flour; conversely, lower-protein flour has a higher percentage of starch, so is considered soft, such as pastry flour (8 to 10 percent protein) or cake flour (6 to 8 percent protein). Neapolitan pizza, as it's made in Italy and now in many wood-fire pizzerias around the world, typically uses 00 flour (the 00 refers to the fineness of the milling) with a hardness closer to that of all-purpose flour (although there are high-protein 00 flours), and thus doesn't need any fat in the dough to tenderize it.

On page 25, you'll find a chart showing which dough I recommend for each type of pizza in the book. In some instances, you might want to modify your version by using a different type of flour or adjusting the amount of oil in it, according to your own taste preferences. There are no hard and fast rules when making such adjustments, other than following the "flavor rule," which you already know means, flavor rules! If it works and you like it, you do not need permission from me or anyone else to tweak as you see fit.

What if I don't have a pizza peel? What's the best way to transfer the pizza onto the baking stone?

A wooden or metal pizza peel is a wonderful tool to have on hand, but it's not the only way to slide a pizza onto a baking stone (or baking steel). I have also used two commonly available tools for this purpose: the back of a regular sheet pan or, alternatively, a wooden cutting board. To expedite the process, I cover the pan or board's surface with a piece of baking parchment, then lightly mist the parchment with pan spray (which makes it easier to move the dough around if it doesn't land on the

exact right spot). The parchment allows the pizza to slide easily off the surface of the pan, parchment and all, onto the baking surface, and the parchment can be easily removed from under the pizza about halfway through the bake. (Note: If you're using a wooden cutting board, you could also flour it as you would a pizza peel, instead of using the parchment paper.)

When removing the pizza from the oven, you can use a metal spatula under the pizza to slide it onto a waiting cutting board.

If you don't have a baking stone or baking steel, you can use the back of a metal sheet pan as the baking platform, preheating it as you would a stone. It may not absorb and radiate heat as efficiently as a stone or steel, but it'll work far better than simply placing the pizza directly into the oven in a cold sheet pan.

A dough series

After mixing the ingredients in either a mixing bowl or in the bowl of an electric mixer to create a coarse, shaggy dough (as described in each dough recipe), rub a teaspoon or two of olive or vegetable oil on the work surface to make an oil slick—the oil will prevent sticking and is for ease of handling. Lift and stretch out the dough and fold it from all sides into the center, pinching and squeezing it closed to form a coarse ball. Lay the dough ball back on the oil slick, seam side down, and flatten it with the palms of your hands and again press and stretch it out and fold it over itself. Pinch and squeeze the seams closed to tighten the dough into a tighter, slightly smoother dough ball. Set it, seam side down, back on the oil slick, and cover it with the bowl to rest for 3 to 5 minutes. Repeat the flattening, stretching, and folding cycle three more times, at 5-minute intervals (the intervals can be as long as 20 minutes). Each stretch-and-fold cycle will cause the dough to become smoother and stronger (that is, tighter and more elastic). Though stronger, the dough should still feel supple and tacky (or even sticky, in the case of the pan pizza dough).

Opening of the dough balls

To open (or stretch) the dough balls into pizza crusts, lightly dust the work surface and the pizza peel with flour to prevent sticking. With floured hands and fingertips, gently tap and flatten the rested dough ball into a round disk of about a 5 to 6-inch diameter. Lift the dough, gently tugging into a circle, and lay it back down on the floured surface. Let the dough relax for 30 to 60 seconds. Flour both the palm and back of your hands and lift the dough, resting it on the back of your hands, with the tips of your thumbs resting on the perimeter edge. Rotate the dough, using your thumbs to gently stretch it out as you turn it. Don't pull the dough with your hands, but let gravity do the work of expanding the circle. The only outward pressure should come from the thumbs, while the backs of your hands support the rest of the dough. When you feel the dough resisting further expansion, lay it back down onto the floured surface and let it rest for 30 to 60 seconds. Then, repeat the opening process with floured hands. It may take three or even four cycles of stretching and resting before the dough expands to the desired diameter (12 to 16 inches, depending on the recipe). When you have achieved the desired diameter, lay the dough on the floured peel, tap it with your fingertips one final time to restore it to the desired diameter (it will likely shrink back when your first lay it down), and begin topping it. Jiggle the peel from time to time to be sure the dough isn't sticking to the peel. If it is, lift and dust under the dough with more flour.

Rolling out dough with a pin for Classic Bar Pizza, Lox and Cream Cheese Pizza on Schmaltz Crust, and Zoli Stromboli

Rub a teaspoon of olive or vegetable oil on the work surface to make an oil slick about 16 inches in diameter. Rub some oil, also, on your hand and fingertips. Transfer the rested dough ball to the oil slick and gently flatten it into a disk with your hand and fingertips. Rub or brush a teaspoon of oil on the top surface of the dough ball to prevent sticking and use a rolling pin (with or without handles) to begin rolling it out. Use minimum downward pressure and always work from the center of the dough to the outer rim, in all directions using short strokes, easing it out gradually to the desired diameter. If the dough shrinks back, you can occasionally lift the dough to release it from the surface and lay it back down onto the lightly oiled work surface to relax before resuming the rolling. For some pizzas, where a rectangle is preferred, roll from the center out to the four corners, and then to the sides, to the size and shape as directed in the specific recipe.

Master Recipes

Pizza Dough Formulas: It's Always First About the Crust

On my pizza quest, I've read many excellent pizza books with many excellent dough recipes, and I've come up with my own dough formulas for different kinds of pizza in my previous books as well. I'm always in search of the perfect crust. An obvious early lesson I learned is that there is no one perfect dough, but instead many perfect doughs. As I gathered the pizzas for this book from the many pizza geniuses I've come to know, my primary challenge was replicating their results without giving away their actual recipes or brands and blends of flour. This is a challenge I've loved tackling.

Since many different styles of pizza are featured in this book, it required creating various dough options—a menu, so to speak, of choices that can be applied as needed. Some doughs are wetter than others, some are leavened by natural wild yeast starters (sourdough) and some with commercial yeast, while others incorporate whole-grain or even nontraditional flours. Rather than create a specific dough for each individual pizza recipe, I created a variety of master dough formulas that cover the full gamut of styles. With these small-batch dough formulas, you should be able to make just about any style of pizza you can imagine, and make killer versions even in regular home ovens. You can make them as they're written, but you're also free to tweak them to your liking should you prefer to vary the flour choices, the hydration, or the fat. The formulas will be given in volume measurements (cups, spoonfuls, and volume), as well as in ounces and grams.

Every pizza in this book has a suggested dough listed in its recipe. In some cases, there may also be a second dough or dough variation listed. However, while these tribute recipes are modeled on an original pizza, the suggested dough comes from one of the versions found in this chapter. You may already have a dough recipe of your own that you'd prefer to use instead, or you may want to use a sourdough version rather than the yeasted dough (or vice versa). The following chart is presented simply to give you a quick reference of my dough suggestions, but the list in no way limits your ability to mix and match or to create your own variations. One of the main goals of this book is to empower you to be creative in the same way as the featured artisan pizza makers, so feel free to consider all the recipes, both doughs and toppings, as starting points for the development of your own versions.

Classic White Dough

Makes 36 ounces (1,021 grams)

21 ounces/595 grams (4⅔ cups) unbleached bread or all-purpose or 00 flour

0.42 ounces/12 grams (1½ teaspoons) kosher salt

0.11 ounces/3 grams (1 teaspoon) instant yeast

14.25 ounces/404 grams water (room temperature, 68° to 72°F)

1 ounce/28 grams olive oil, plus more for greasing (optional)

In a mixing bowl or the bowl of an electric mixer, stir together the flour, salt, and yeast. Add the water and stir with a large spoon, or use the paddle attachment and mix on slow speed for 30 seconds to form a coarse, shaggy dough. Add the oil, if using. Increase the speed to medium (or continue mixing with the spoon or with wet hands) and mix for an additional 30 to 60 seconds to make a wet, coarse, sticky dough. Let the dough rest for 5 minutes to fully hydrate.

If using an electric mixer, switch to the dough hook. Increase the mixer to medium-high speed (or continue mixing by hand) and mix for an additional 2 to 4 minutes to make a smooth dough, adding more flour or water if needed. The dough should be soft and supple, very tacky but not sticky to the touch, and offer a little resistance when pressed with a wet finger.

Use 1 teaspoon of oil to make a 15-inch diameter oil slick on the work surface. Rub oil on a plastic bowl scraper and on your hands, then use the scraper to transfer the dough to the oil slick. Stretch and fold the dough (see page 16). Invert the mixing bowl and use it to cover the dough. Let it rest for 2 to 5 minutes. Repeat the stretch and fold, rubbing additional oil on the work surface as needed. Cover the dough again, let it rest for 2 to 5 minutes, and repeat the stretch and fold. Cover with the bowl and again let it rest for 2 to 5 minutes. Perform one final stretch and fold to make a smooth ball of dough. The dough will have firmed up after each stretch and fold and should now be smooth, supple, and tacky to the touch, but not sticky.

Place the dough into a lightly oiled bowl or container, roll it around to coat with oil, then cover the bowl with plastic wrap and refrigerate it for anywhere from 12 to 72 hours.

On the day you plan to bake, remove dough from the refrigerator 3 hours before baking, or as directed in the pizza recipe. Immediately divide it into the desired size pieces and round them into balls. Line a sheet pan with lightly oiled baking parchment or a silicone baking mat, then place the dough balls on it. Mist them with vegetable oil spray and cover the pan with plastic wrap or a plastic can liner. Then follow the recipe according to the type of pizza you're making.

Notes

- You can substitute up to 25 percent whole-grain or other flour (such as semolina, rye, heirloom, etc.) for an equal amount of white flour, but increase the water by 0.5 ounces (14 grams) for every 2 ounces (57 grams) of whole-grain flour you swap in.

- Omit the olive oil in dough for wood-fired, high-heat pizzas, such as pure Neapolitan-style, and increase the water by 1 ounce (28 g).

- You can use any brand of vegetable or olive oil spray to lightly oil the bowls and dough balls.

- Use all-purpose flour or 00 Italian flour for Neapolitan-style pizza, and bread flour for neo-Neapolitan (or Neapolitan-ish) pizzas, whether baking in home ovens or wood-fired ovens.

- With some brands of flour, you may need to increase or decrease the water amount. Always let the dough dictate how much it needs, using the recipe as a general guideline.

Pan Pizza Dough

Makes 38 ounces (1,077 grams)

21 ounces/595 grams (4⅔ cups) unbleached bread flour

0.42 ounces/12 grams (1½ teaspoons) kosher salt

0.11 ounces/3 grams (1 teaspoon) instant yeast

17 ounces/482 grams water (room temperature, 68° to 72°F)

1 ounce/28 grams olive oil

In a mixing bowl or the bowl of an electric mixer, stir together the flour, salt, and yeast. Add the water and stir with a large spoon, or use the paddle attachment and mix on slow speed for 30 seconds to form a coarse, shaggy dough. Add the oil. Increase the speed to medium (or continue mixing with the spoon or with wet hands) and mix for an additional 30 to 60 seconds to make a wet, coarse, sticky dough. Let the dough rest for 5 minutes to fully hydrate.

Increase the mixer to medium-high speed (still using the paddle, or continue mixing by hand) and mix for 30 more seconds to make a smooth, sticky dough. It should be soft, supple, wet and sticky to the touch, and offer a little resistance when pressed with a wet finger.

Use 1 teaspoon of oil to make a 15-inch diameter oil slick on the work surface. Rub oil on a plastic bowl scraper and on your hands, then use the scraper to transfer the dough to the oil slick. Stretch and fold the dough (see page 16). Invert the mixing bowl and use it to cover the dough. Let it rest for 2 to 5 minutes. Repeat the stretch and fold, rubbing additional oil on the work surface as needed. Cover the dough again, let it rest for 2 to 5 minutes, and repeat the stretch and fold. Cover with the bowl and again let it rest for 2 to 5 minutes. Perform one final stretch and fold to make a smooth ball of dough. The dough will have firmed up after each stretch and fold and will now be soft, smooth, supple, and slightly sticky, but firm enough to hold together when lifted.

Place the dough into a lightly oiled bowl, cover it with plastic wrap, and refrigerate it for anywhere from 12 to 72 hours.

On the day you plan to bake, remove the dough from the refrigerator 4 to 5 hours before baking and follow the steps for panning according to the type of pizza you're making.

Notes

- You can substitute up to 25 percent whole-grain or other flour (such as semolina, rye, heirloom, etc.) for an equal amount of white flour, but increase the water by 0.5 ounces (14 grams) for every 2 ounces (57 grams) of whole-grain flour you swap in.

- You can use any brand of vegetable or olive oil spray to lightly oil the bowls and dough balls.

- With some brands of flour, you may need to increase or decrease the water amount. Always let the dough dictate how much it needs, using the recipe as a general guideline.

New York Pizza Dough

Makes 36 ounces (1,021 grams)

21 ounces/595 grams (4⅔ cups) unbleached high-gluten flour or unbleached bread flour

0.42 ounces/12 grams (1½ teaspoons) kosher salt

0.11 ounces/3 grams (1 teaspoon) instant yeast

1 ounce/28 grams (2 tablespoons) sugar, brown sugar, or honey

13 ounces/369 grams water (room temperature, 68° to 72°F) *

1.5 ounces/43 grams olive oil

*For the Bar Pizza (page 98), reduce the water to 12 ounces (340 grams) to make a stiffer dough

In a mixing bowl or the bowl of an electric mixer, stir together the flour, salt, yeast, and sugar. Add the water and stir with a large spoon, or use the paddle attachment and mix on slow speed for 3 minutes to form a coarse, shaggy dough.

Add the oil. Increase the speed to medium (or continue mixing with the spoon or with wet hands) and mix for an additional 2 to 3 minutes to make a coarse, tacky dough. If there is any unabsorbed flour, add more water, 1 teaspoon at a time, during mixing. Let the dough rest for 5 minutes to fully hydrate. Extra water may be required if high-gluten flour is used.

If using an electric mixer, increase the speed to medium-high (or continue mixing by hand) and mix for another 2 to 3 minutes to make a smooth dough, adding more flour or water if needed. It should be soft, supple, and only slightly tacky—or even satiny—to the touch, and should offer resistance and a spring-back quality when pressed with a wet finger.

Use 1 teaspoon of oil to make a 15-inch diameter oil slick on the work surface. Rub oil on a plastic bowl scraper and on your hands, then use the scraper to transfer the dough to the oil slick. Stretch and fold the dough 1 time (see page 16). The dough should now be smooth, supple, and satiny to the touch.

Lightly oil a bowl or container and place the dough into it, then cover it with plastic wrap and refrigerate it for anywhere from 12 to 72 hours.

On the day you plan to bake, remove the dough from the refrigerator 3 hours before baking, or as described in pizza recipe. Immediately divide it into the desired size pieces and round them into balls. Line a sheet pan with lightly oiled baking parchment or a silicone baking mat, then place the dough balls on the pan. Mist them with vegetable oil spray and cover the pan with plastic wrap or a plastic can liner. Then follow the recipe according to the type of pizza you're making.

Notes

- You can substitute up to 25 percent whole-grain or other flour (such as semolina, rye, heirloom, etc.) for an equal amount of white flour, but increase the water by 0.5 ounces (14 grams) for every 2 ounces (57 grams) of whole-grain flour you swap in.

- You can use any brand of vegetable or olive oil spray to lightly oil the bowls and dough balls.

- With some brands of flour, you may need to increase or decrease the water amount. Always let the dough dictate how much it needs, using the recipe as a general guideline.

Sourdough Pizza Dough

Makes 37 ounces (1,048 grams)

16 ounces/454 grams (3½ cups) unbleached high-gluten flour, unbleached bread flour, or all-purpose flour, depending on the type of pizza you're making

0.42 ounces/12 grams (1½ teaspoons) kosher salt

0.11 ounces/3 grams (1 teaspoon) instant yeast (optional, for "mixed or spiked" method. See page 13)

8 ounces/227 grams sourdough starter (page 36)

11 ounces/312 grams water (room temperature, 68° to 72°F) (If making pan pizza, use 13.5 ounces/383 grams.)

1.5 ounces/43 grams olive oil (If making wood-fired Neapolitan pizza, omit the oil.)

In a mixing bowl or the bowl of an electric mixer, stir together the flour, salt, and instant yeast (if using). Add the sourdough starter and the water and stir with a large spoon, or use the paddle attachment and mix on slow speed for 3 to 4 minutes to form a coarse, shaggy dough.

Add the oil, if using. Increase the speed to medium (or continue mixing with the spoon or with wet hands) and mix for an additional 2 to 4 minutes to make a coarse, tacky dough. If there is any unabsorbed flour, add more water, 1 teaspoon at a time, during mixing. Extra water may be required if high-gluten flour is used. Let the dough rest for 5 minutes to fully hydrate.

If using an electric mixer, increase the speed to medium-high (or continue mixing by hand) and mix for another 2 to 3 minutes to make a smooth dough, adding more flour or water if needed. The dough should be supple and only slightly tacky—or even satiny— to the touch, and offer resistance and a spring-back quality when pressed with a wet finger.

Use 1 teaspoon of oil to make a 15-inch diameter oil slick on the work surface. Rub oil on a plastic bowl scraper and on your hands, then use the scraper to transfer the dough to the oil slick. Stretch and fold the dough 1 time (see page 16). The dough will now be smooth, supple, and slightly tacky to the touch. If the dough is still not smooth and easy to handle, repeat the stretch and fold process 1 or 2 additional times, with 2-minute resting periods in between.

Lightly oil a bowl or other container and place the dough into it. Roll the dough around to coat it with the oil, then cover with plastic wrap. If using straight sourdough and no commercial yeast, leave the dough at room temperature for 2 to 4 hours, until it begins to swell in size, then refrigerate it for anywhere from 12 to 72 hours. If using the mixed method (with commercial yeast), refrigerate the dough immediately.

On the day you plan to bake, remove the dough from the refrigerator 3 hours before baking, or as directed in pizza recipe. Immediately divide it into the desired size pieces and round them into balls. Line a sheet pan with lightly oiled baking parchment or a silicone baking mat. Place the dough balls on the pan and mist them with vegetable oil spray, then cover the pan with plastic wrap or a plastic can liner. Then follow the recipe according to the type of pizza you're making.

Notes

- This recipe calls for 50 percent sourdough starter to 100 percent new flour in the final dough. This is a higher proportion of flour to starter than many recipes, and if you are an experienced sourdough baker, you may want to reduce the percentage of starter to flour to as low as 15 percent, or 25 or 33 percent. There is no fixed rule, though the amount of salt may need to be slightly reduced if you reduce the amount of starter, and the fermentation times may vary. This recipe is designed to provide maximum sourdough flavor and complexity even if you use the yeast-spiking method (see page 13). If you have a preferred version of sourdough pizza crust, feel free to use it in the recipes that call for a sourdough crust.

- If you already have a sourdough mother starter that's kept at a higher hydration rate than the one described in this book, feel free to use it, but remember to reduce the water in the dough by an appropriate amount to achieve the described texture.

- You can substitute up to 25 percent whole-grain or other flour (such as semolina, rye, heirloom, etc.) for an equal amount of white flour, but increase the water by 0.5 ounces (14 grams) for every 2 ounces (57 grams) of whole-grain flour you swap in.

- You can use any brand of vegetable or olive oil spray to lightly oil the bowls and dough balls.

- With some brands of flour, you may need to increase or decrease the water amount. Always let the dough dictate how much it needs, using the recipe as a general guideline.

Variations: Other Grains or Ingredients

Some of the pizza recipes in this book suggest adjustments or tweaks to the four foundational master doughs offered. Even if a dough doesn't call for a tweak, you're always free to adjust it according to your taste or intuition. Here are some ideas for possible tweaks:

- The amount of oil can vary in some instances. The master dough recipes use about 4.75 percent to 7 percent oil to flour (by weight), but there are times when no oil is required or oil in excess of 7 percent might be appropriate. The type of flour is a factor in determining the amount of oil or fat required; for instance, high-gluten (high-protein) flour absorbs more water than bread flour or all-purpose flour and is also more chewy, as the protein is in excess of 14 percent of the total flour, so additional oil is used to help tenderize it.

- The type of fat is not limited to olive or vegetable oil. Aside from flavor, the primary function of fat in dough is to tenderize it and to help retain moisture during the bake, as well as to enhance flavor. One recipe (page 74) specifically calls for chicken fat (schmaltz), and there is certainly no reason you can't use schmaltz or bacon or pork fat, or even beef tallow, if you'd like to experiment.

- Many alternative flours are now available, including non-wheat flours such as corn, rye, millet, barley, buckwheat, sorghum, and teff. Heirloom strains of wheat (einkorn, emmer, Khorasan, etc.) and other grains are also available and, while more expensive than standard flour, often provide subtle flavor and texture benefits. My suggestion is to use them sparingly (25 percent or less of the total flour) until you become familiar with their properties and functionality, then increase the percentages as you become comfortable with them.

- The master doughs in this book are mainly white-flour–based and perform like white-flour crusts, even when whole-grain flour is swapped in (if the percentage of whole-grain flour is less than 25 percent of the total flour). However, there is no rule about using more whole-grain flour, even up to 100 percent, but be aware that whole-grain flour requires a higher percentage of water. My rule of thumb is 0.5 ounces/14 grams of additional water (1 tablespoon of water for every 2 ounces, or 57 grams, of whole-grain flour), but there are exceptions to this guideline. When swapping in whole-wheat flour, I suggest using sprouted whole-wheat flour, which is available at many supermarkets. It is naturally sweeter and also easier to digest.

- You can also use cooked grains in the doughs, such as oatmeal, polenta, and brown rice or cooked barley. These grains, when cooked as porridges, add a lot of moisture, texture, and flavor to your crust, but they do work against the usual expansion (or oven spring) of the dough during the bake, creating airy, puffy corniciones (the exposed edge of the crust). These are the kind of swap-outs that you may want to try after first mastering the foundational formulas.

- I will never dissuade you from using organically grown flour and other organic ingredients when you can get them—and I encourage their use whenever possible—but the performance of these doughs is not dependent on organic flour.

Sourdough Starter from Scratch

There are many ways to make a sourdough starter from scratch, and I've provided a different method in every one of my bread and pizza books to date. I've learned, over the years, that keeping it simple is the best approach, so what follows is the distillation of a number of previous versions. If you already have a starter going, there's no need to make a new one for the recipes in this book; all you need to do is refresh the mother starter you already have to build a fresh final starter for your pizza dough. Just remember this, and you'll have a solid foundation: A sourdough starter is a medium in which wild yeast and bacterial microorganisms live and thrive together and, as a favor to us, produce alcohol, lactic acid, and acetic acid for flavor, as well as carbon dioxide, which raises the dough. It is at once natural, scientific, and miraculous.

Using the following method, you'll first create a seed culture full of a growing community of wild yeast and bacteria. Then you'll expand that into a mother starter, which you can keep going indefinitely by feeding it, before you run out, to build it back to your desired volume.

For the seed culture, I always suggest the use of a small amount of either pineapple or orange juice for the liquid on Day 1. This is explained in more detail in my other books, but the short explanation is that the acidity in the juice helps shorten the time to get the process started. Wild yeast cells prefer a somewhat acidic pH environment in which to grow, and some bacteria mimic yeast activity at more neutral pH levels, fooling us into thinking the starter is ready before it actually is. The juice is not required, as the starter will work with just water if you're patient, but it has become a trusted method. The juice is used only on Day 1; after that, use water only.

Day 1

2.25 ounces/64 grams (½ cup) of flour, either unbleached bread flour or whole wheat

1.5 ounces/43 grams pineapple juice, orange juice, or water, cool or at room temperature

Place the flour and liquid into a glass or stainless steel bowl and use a spoon to mix them, forming a small piece of dough, slightly sticky or tacky (similar in structure to bread dough). Dust the work surface with flour and knead the dough for a few seconds to hydrate all the flour, but don't worry about developing the gluten. Wash or wipe out the mixing bowl, mist it lightly with vegetable oil spray, and place the dough back in. Cover the bowl loosely with plastic wrap or a lid and leave it at room temperature for about 24 hours.

Day 2

Knead the dough in the bowl or on a flour-dusted work surface for about 30 seconds to aerate it and redistribute the ingredients. There should be little or no fermentation activity at this point (if, for some reason, the dough has expanded to double in size, you can move on to the next phase, though this is unlikely). Return the piece to the covered container and leave it at room temperature for another 24 hours.

Day 3

4.5 ounces/128 grams (1 cup) unbleached
   bread flour

3 ounces/85 grams water, room temperature

There may or may not be any signs of
fermentation or bubbling; regardless, add this
new flour and water into the dough and stir for
about 30 seconds with a large spoon or rubber
spatula, then knead on a floured work surface
for about 1 minute to make a smooth dough ball.
Wipe out the container again (dough residue on
the walls of the bowl can dry out and become
crusty and is more vulnerable to mold-forming
bacteria). Lightly mist the bowl with oil spray and
place the dough in it. Cover the bowl loosely
with plastic wrap or a lid and leave it at room
temperature for 8 hours. Then knead the dough
again to aerate it, cover it in the container as
before, and leave it at room temperature for 8 to
24 hours.

Day 4 or 5—the Mother Starter

1 cup (4.5 ounces/128 grams) unbleached bread
   flour

3 ounces/85 grams water

There's a good likelihood that the dough will
show some signs of fermentation by Day 4
(bubbling; alcohol, buttermilk, or acidic aromas;
expansion in size). If not, knead the dough
and return it to the container and add the
flour and water on Day 5 regardless of signs of
fermentation.

If there's active fermentation on Day 4, stir in the flour and water and knead into a ball as described previously, then return it to a covered bowl. Cover the container loosely and leave at room temperature. Knead the dough twice a day until the dough comes to life, actively fermenting, creating bubbles, and doubling in size. It should develop a pleasant, acidic aroma, similar to apple cider. This could take anywhere from 1 to 8 days (the length of time will depend on your climate, the time of year, and the ambient temperature of your kitchen—a few degrees' difference can affect the rate of this initial fermentation development by as many as 3 or 4 days). If there's little or no activity during the initial days, don't give up. The frequent kneading will prevent the dough from getting moldy and will encourage the growth of the right kind of microorganisms.

When the starter comes to life and doubles in size, immediately knead it, return it to the container, cover the container more tightly, and refrigerate it. It's now ready to use and will become the "mother starter" from which future pizza dough—and also bread dough—can be made. You should have about 18 ounces of sourdough starter—more than enough to start making pizza dough.

Note: As a general rule, it takes 2 or 3 refreshment cycles for a sourdough starter to reach its full potency. For that reason, I'd suggest that the first time you use this new starter in a pizza dough, you use the "spike" method (see page 13) to guarantee success. However, if your mother starter seems active and potent right from the get-go, you can, of course, try it out without the added yeast, though you should be prepared for slower rising times.

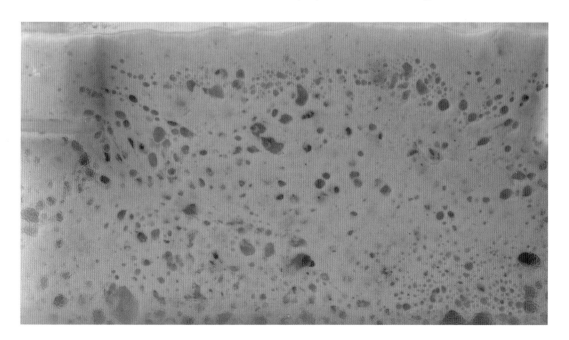

Refreshing the Starter

Once a mother starter has been unused for more than 4 or 5 days, it begins to break down due to the action of acids and enzyme activity on the protein and starch chains. The dough will begin to lose its structural integrity, but it can still work as leavening in a pizza dough for up to 7 days (and sometimes longer). The microorganisms are still viable, but if you use it in your final dough, it can weaken the overall structure, so it must first be refreshed. The easiest way to refresh a starter is by simply adding more flour and water to it at the same 66 percent hydration ratio as in the beginning.

If you're using up your starter quickly and need to rebuild it within 6 days, you can use a 1-to-1 build (equal parts new flour and starter), but if the starter has not been refreshed for 7 days or more, you should use a 2-to-1 build. If it's going longer than 3 weeks without refreshment, build it by adding flour at 3 to 1 (triple the weight of flour to starter). You can discard some of the old starter, since you may not need to triple it all if you have a lot of unused starter.

Some clarifications

For a 2-to-1 build, if you have 8 ounces (227 grams) of old starter, you would add 16 ounces (454 grams) of bread flour plus 10.5 ounces (298 grams) of water (66 percent of 16 ounces), and then allow 4 to 8 hours for it to ferment and become a new, stronger mother starter, weighing about 2 pounds. If you don't want to keep that much starter on hand, discard some of the old starter and build it back with, say, 4 ounces (113 grams) of starter, 8 ounces (227 grams) of flour and 5.25 ounces (149 grams) of water (66 percent water to flour).

However, in instances where the mother starter hasn't been used for 30 days or more, I prefer to refresh it at a ratio of 4 times the amount of flour to starter, because the original mother starter is so compromised it needs much more new flour to refresh it. In instances like this, it might take longer for the newly refreshed starter to ferment—perhaps 6 to 12 hours—so you have to plan accordingly. Also, feeding the starter at this ratio can quickly gobble up a lot of flour and produce more mother starter than you need (unless you're making large batches

of pizza dough or bread). So it might be better to weigh out a small amount of this old mother starter, say 2 ounces (57 grams), and add 8 ounces (227 grams) of flour plus 5.25 ounces (149 grams) of water (66 percent of the flour weight). This will produce about 15 ounces of new starter, which is probably enough for most situations, since you need only 8 ounces of starter in your single-batch recipes. (Note: When pulling out a small amount of old starter to make a new mother starter, hold on to the remaining old starter as insurance or backup, at least until the new mother starter proves itself viable. Once the new starter is up and running, you can discard the old mother starter.)

Final Notes

- For those wishing for a more sour taste, the addition of a small amount of sugar (2 percent to 3 percent of the flour weight), either when refreshing the starter itself or in the final dough, fosters the development of bacteria that produce more acetic, sour flavors. If you prefer less sourness or tang, use the instant yeast "spike" in your final dough in addition to the starter, to reduce fermentation time and, thus, reduce the development of acid-producing bacteria.

- Once your mother starter is established, or refreshed, you should store it in a clean container—whether plastic, glass, or ceramic—with a tight-fitting lid or plastic wrap to prevent air from drying the surface or exposing it to extraneous microorganisms in the refrigerator. It's best to use a new or cleaned container after each refreshment. If you're leaving the starter dormant in the refrigerator for weeks or months, be sure the inner walls of the container are scraped back down into the main dough with a wet rubber spatula, or transfer the dough to a clean container.

...shed Tomato Pizza Sauce

Makes 4 cups

Pizza sauce is a crucial aspect of any pizzeria's repertoire, and many places have built their reputations on their sauces as much as on their crusts. There are plenty of debates regarding the merits of Italian-grown San Marzano tomatoes and California or even New Jersey-grown versions of the same variety, so if you have a brand or recipe preference, by all means use it. Some pizzerias that make more than one style of pizza, such as Tony's Pizza Napoletana, will even bring in tomato products from a number of different distributors to pair with the specific pizzas on which they will be used.

My experience, especially for pizzas made at home, is that many excellent brands in supermarkets or local grocers will work on the pizzas in this book, so rather than specify for each recipe, I've chosen to give you one recipe that always delivers the goods, and I'll leave the brand of tomatoes up to you. The point is, the pizza will be great either way. The one caveat is that each brand has its own tomato density and salt content, so it will be up to you to make final tweaks to your taste. Otherwise, the following recipe can be used on any pizza in this book unless otherwise stipulated. You aren't likely to use the whole batch if making only a few pizzas, but the good news is that you can keep the remaining sauce in the refrigerator for up to 3 weeks, or simply freeze it.

28-ounce (794-gram) can whole, ground, crushed, or diced tomatoes

¼ teaspoon black pepper

1 teaspoon dried basil, or 2 tablespoons minced fresh basil

¼ teaspoon dried oregano, or 1 teaspoon minced fresh oregano

1 teaspoon granulated garlic, or 3 to 4 cloves fresh garlic, minced

1 tablespoon red wine vinegar or freshly squeezed lemon juice

½ to 1 teaspoon kosher salt (depending on the brand of tomatoes)

If using crushed or ground tomatoes, place all ingredients except salt in a bowl and mix with a large spoon or whisk. Taste, then add salt as needed.

If using whole, chopped, or diced tomatoes, place all ingredients except salt in a food processor with the blade attachment and process for 15 to 20 seconds. Check the consistency. If it is still too chunky, pulse as many times as it takes to crush or grind the tomatoes to the texture of coarse sand. Taste and add salt or water as needed. The sauce will thicken slightly as it rests.

Keep the finished sauce in a covered container in the refrigerator, where it will be good for up to 3 weeks, or freeze it for future use, thawing it slowly at room temperature or overnight in the refrigerator.

Notes

- You can buy whole canned tomatoes, as well as diced, pureed, or crushed (also known as ground tomatoes). Ground or crushed is preferred over pureed, because those little bits of tomato solids provide wonderful texture. That said, if all you have is tomato puree, go ahead and use it. You can also make your own crushed tomatoes from whole or diced tomatoes by simply pulsing them in a food processor. Use the brand or type you like most and turn them into the crushed tomato sauce that follows, and you'll be good to go. If you want to make your sauce thicker, add a small amount of tomato paste and adjust the salt to taste. Most of the time this won't be necessary unless you have a particularly juicy brand of tomatoes.

- Pizza sauce rarely needs to be cooked in advance, since the tomatoes are already cooked during the canning process. If you want to use this sauce for pasta or to cook meatballs or sausage, then yes, heat it up; but if it's going on pizza, whether before or after it's baked, there's no need.

- If you have my other pizza books, you'll notice that this recipe looks very familiar. That's because, frankly, I am so pleased with it and receive so many compliments from home cooks as well as restaurants that use it, that I stand pat on this one. However, many of you have your own personal or family recipe, and I take no offense if you prefer to use it instead. Pizza is, among its many attributes, very personal, and as I said in the introduction, the recipes throughout this book should be viewed as guidelines to jump-start your own creativity, whether it be with the cheese, dough, or sauce.

Hoagie Spread

Only a couple of pizzas in this collection call for hoagie spread as an ingredient, but I believe you will use it on many of them anyway, which is why this recipe is included. Hoagies—and all sandwiches, for that matter—have a lot in common with pizza. After all, a pizza is dough with something on it, and a sandwich is dough with something in it. Hoagie spread is a kind of secret sauce, and every good hoagie shop has its own version, whether a simple oil and vinegar splash or something more elaborate, like the one here.

A couple of decent supermarket brands are available if you don't want to make your own (Haddon House, for one, as well as the Cento brand), but I find a lot of joy in making this and having it on hand for all sorts of uses, the main ones being just about any type of sandwich and many types of pizzas. The only recipe in this book that specifically calls for it is the Zoli Stromboli (page 165), which is, after all, a type of pizza hoagie. But as many people have discovered with hot honey (called for in a number of pizzas in this book but not restricted to those), this hoagie spread, with its spice, vinegar, and garlic acidity, will make flavors pop (or zing) on almost any version of pizza.

1 cup pickled cherry peppers, stemmed

1 cup pepperoncini peppers, stemmed*

3 to 4 garlic cloves, peeled

1 red bell pepper, stemmed and seeded, cut into about 6 pieces, or 1 or 2 Fresno, Anaheim, or red jalapeño or serrano peppers for a spicier version

1 tablespoon olive oil

¼ cup brine from the pepperoncini or the cherry peppers

¼ cup red wine vinegar, plus extra for added seasoning

Salt

Place all ingredients except the salt in a food processor and process for 20 to 30 seconds to fully break down the peppers and garlic for a relish-like consistency. If still not broken down, pulse as many times as needed to do so. Taste and add salt or more vinegar, if needed. Keep refrigerated in a covered container when not using; it will keep for at least 3 months.

*You can also add pickled jalapeño peppers in addition to or instead of the pepperoncini, if you like it spicier.

Note: You can control the spicy heat level by your choice of peppers. If you like it mild, use fresh red bell peppers; for medium, red Fresno or Anaheim peppers; and for spicy, red jalapeños or serrano peppers, or a blend of them all. You can always use hotter peppers if you like, but remember that this is a garnish, so it should enhance the main ingredients—not overwhelm them. In our house, we keep both a mild and spicy version on hand.

By the way, the pickled cherry peppers are an important—not optional—ingredient. They have a little zing and are not overly spicy, but they really are the defining ingredient.

The
Pizzas

Round
Pies

The Ultimate White Pie with Garlic Confit

Makes 4 (12-inch) pizzas

Nino Coniglio is the founder of Williamsburg Pizza in Brooklyn, as well as the front man for the Brooklyn Pizza Crew, who have been making fun pizza videos for the past few years. Nino is a competition champion and amazingly prolific as a creator of new pizza concepts. He and his wife, Shealyn (as a team they are a dynamic force of nature), live in the Bushwick section of Brooklyn, where they've been baking and giving away pizzas from the outdoor oven in their front yard to their neighbors throughout the pandemic.

Here's how Shealyn described their Ultimate White Pie to me:

I would say that what's special about this pie is that when the pandemic began Nino was convinced the world was ending, so he planted a garden out back and now we are reaping the benefits and putting our home-grown ingredients on our pizzas. Nino believes in quality ingredients from start to finish—not only because it tastes better but because it's better for your health! He likes to tell people that he ferments his dough long enough to where it's actually good for you and has more probiotics than yogurt.

During quarantine we also started the Brooklyn Pizza Club out of our home, partly as a way to supplement our income but, also, to give back to the neighborhood by delivering pies one day a week to essential workers that live or work near our block. Pizza is our way of spreading positivity and love, which I think is what we've all needed this year!

I agree, it's hard to beat home-grown ingredients, but don't let that stop you from making this pizza with store-bought or farmer's market ingredients. Just be creative and thoughtful about your ingredients like Nino and Shealyn are, and you'll be following the spirit, if not the letter, of their inspiration.

Sourdough Pizza Dough (page 32), made at least a day ahead

4 ounces (113 grams) olive oil

24 cloves garlic, peeled and coarsely chopped

⅛ teaspoon kosher or sea salt

White Sauce (recipe follows)

2 cups cherry or grape tomatoes, cut in half

1 cup freshly grated Grana Padano or Parmesan cheese

16 ounces (454 grams) cupping pepperoni slices or standard size slices cut in half

1 cup tightly packed fresh basil leaves

Coarse or flake sea salt (such as Sicilian)

Salt and freshly ground black pepper

16 ounces (454 grams) fresh mozzarella (fior di latte), cut or torn into 1-inch pieces

Remove the dough from the refrigerator 4 hours before baking, or 3 hours before baking if using the yeast "spike" mixed method (see page 13). Weigh out and shape 4 dough balls of 9 ounces (255 grams) each. Mist a sheet pan or dough box with vegetable or olive oil spray and place the dough balls on the pan. Mist the tops lightly with the oil spray, then cover the pan or dough box loosely with plastic wrap. Set aside at room temperature to proof for 3 to 4 hours.

For the garlic confit, heat the olive oil in a small saucepan until a few drops of water sizzle and splatter when sprinkled into the pan. Immediately remove the pan from the heat and stir in the chopped garlic. Stir in the salt and set the pan aside to cool at room temperature.

An hour before making the pizzas, place a baking stone or baking steel on the middle oven rack and preheat to 550°F or as hot the oven will allow. When it's time to bake the pizzas, begin stretching the dough balls (see page 18) to 11 to 12 inches in diameter. Assemble one pizza at a time, preparing the next pizza while the previous one is baking.

Lightly dust a pizza peel with flour or semolina. Transfer one stretched dough onto the pizza peel. Spread one-fourth of the white sauce over the surface of the dough, leaving a border of about ¼ inch around the outer edge without sauce. Evenly distribute ½ cup of the sliced tomatoes over the surface. Sprinkle 2 tablespoons of the grated Grana Padano over the tomatoes, then evenly distribute ½ cup of the pepperoni slices over the whole pizza.

Slide the pizza onto the baking stone and bake for 4 minutes. Rotate 180 degrees and continue baking an additional 2 to 4 minutes, until the crust is golden brown around the edge and on the underside, the tomatoes are sizzling, the cheese is caramelized and bubbly, and the pepperoni have curled into cups and crisped up. Remove the pizza from the oven and transfer it to a cutting board. Coarsely chop one-quarter of the fresh basil and distribute it over the tomatoes. Drizzle 2 tablespoons of the garlic confit over the surface, followed by 2 tablespoons of the Grana Padano, as well as coarse sea salt and ground black pepper to taste. Slice and serve while making the next pizza.

White Sauce

8 ounces (227 grams) mascarpone cheese

8 ounces (227 grams) ricotta cheese

4 ounces (113 grams) fresh buffalo mozzarella (or substitute fior di latte)

Puree mascarpone, ricotta, and buffalo mozzarella in a blender, food processor, or electric mixer. Add salt and pepper to taste. Transfer the sauce into a small bowl, cover with plastic wrap, and refrigerate until needed.

Brian Spangler

Clams Casino Pizza, Portland-Style

Makes 3 (14-inch) pizzas

Brian Spangler, founder and proprietor of Apizza Scholls in Portland, Oregon, is the most frequent guest, along with John Arena, on our show, *Pizza Talk*. Together, Brian and John form the nucleus of our so-called board of pizza elders, whom we affectionately refer to as the Pizza Yodi's. Brian and I have known each other for many years, predating our immersion in the pizza world, going back to when we were artisan bread bakery owners and active board members of The Bread Bakers Guild of America.

Eventually, Brian took his dough knowledge into the pizza sector and created a destination restaurant that was Portland's local little secret until Anthony Bourdain discovered Apizza Scholls and put it on the world map via his television show *Anthony Bourdain: No Reservations,* as well as in a book where he talks about this pizza. While Anthony was there, after a long day of filming—and while relaxing over more than a couple of cold ones—he and Brian bonded over their passion for clam pizza, so Brian created this one for him.

Unlike the famous Frank Pepe's white clam pie of New Haven, this one leaves the clams in the shell, where their juices spill out over the surface during the bake, immersing the pie with clam essence. Of course, it's the bacon, garlic, and chili flakes that make it a "clams casino," but the other thing that separates this clam-in-the-shell pie from any other I've had is the sheer abundance of clams. As Brian told me, "I'm not gonna tease you with 6 or 7 clams like everyone else does. If I'm making a clam pizza, you can damn well be sure it will be a friggin' clam festival!" (Note: If you know Brian, you also know that he didn't say "friggin'.")

24 ounces (680 grams) sliced bacon

New York Pizza Dough (page 30), made at least a day ahead

Spice Blend

1 head garlic, peeled and minced

4 teaspoons dried chili flakes

1 tablespoon dried oregano

1 tablespoon dried basil

1 tablespoon dried parsley, or 3 tablespoons minced fresh parsley

1 teaspoon dried marjoram or thyme

½ teaspoon kosher salt

¼ teaspoon black pepper

45 Manila or cherrystone clams, in the shell

8 ounces (227 grams) Parmesan or Grana Padano cheese, grated (about 4 cups)

½ cup diced Italian parsley (for garnish)

The day before baking (or earlier the day of baking), preheat the oven to 400°F and lay out the strips of bacon on 2 (12 by 18-inch) sheet pans. Bake for 10 to 15 minutes, until the bacon is about three-quarters cooked, just beginning to brown but still limp. Remove the pans from the oven and set them on the stovetop so the bacon can cool in its own fat. When the bacon strips have fully cooled, remove them from the pans and cut them in half crosswise to make shorter strips, then stack them on a paper towel-covered plate. Cover the plate with plastic wrap and chill until assembly. Save any residual bacon fat in a jar or container for later use.

Three hours before baking, remove the dough from the refrigerator. Divide it into 3 (12-ounce/340-gram) pieces, then form the pieces into tight dough balls. Lightly mist a sheet pan or dough box with vegetable oil spray and place the dough balls on the pan or in the dough box. Mist the top of the dough balls with the oil spray and cover loosely with plastic wrap. Set aside to proof at room temperature for about 3 hours.

While the dough is rising, assemble the toppings and blend the spices. Wash the clams and scrub them of all sand, draining off any excess water.

An hour before making the pizzas, place the baking stone or baking steel on the middle oven rack and preheat to 550°F, or as hot as the oven allows.

When it's time to bake the pizzas, make one at a time by stretching out a dough ball to about 14 inches in diameter (see page 18). Lightly dust a pizza peel with flour, semolina, or cornmeal and lay the dough on the peel. Distribute one-third of the grated cheese over the surface (about 1⅓ cup), leaving a ½-inch border around the outer edge without cheese. Then distribute ⅓ of the spice mixture over the cheese. Lay out 15 clams over the surface, then drape ⅓ of the partly cooked bacon strips over the clams. Make sure the pizza slides easily on the peel; if not, dust additional flour underneath the crust.

Slide the pizza onto the baking stone and bake for 4 minutes. Rotate 180 degrees and continue baking for an additional 2 to 4 minutes, until the crust is golden brown around the edge and on the underside. The clams will have opened, with the juices dripping over the cheese and into the crust. Transfer the pizza to a cutting board and garnish with ⅓ of the chopped parsley. Slice and serve while you make the next pie. (Be sure to provide an empty bowl for the shells!)

Jonathan Goldsmith

"Ben Essere"

Makes 4 (12-inch) pizzas

Jonathan Goldsmith, padrone of the internationally beloved Spacca Napoli Pizzeria in Chicago, has had a long and interesting journey, including stints as a social worker, opera lover, and property manager, all of which ultimately led him to his true passion and calling—traditional Neapolitan pizza. He shared this journey with us, including his years living and learning in Italy, on a memorable episode of *Pizza Talk* and offered this very special (not on the menu) pizza for inclusion in the book. As Jonathan tells it, he created this one for Antimo Caputo, don of the famous Caputo Flour family, as a way to incorporate and showcase other grains and seeds.

My tribute version here is not nearly as complex as Jonathan's, which included flax, sesame, and sunflower seeds as well as barley, rye, and wheat. You can use the recipe below as a starting point if you'd like to experiment, but bear in mind Jonathan's advice to keep the additional grains and seeds to no more than 7.5 percent of the total flour weight, or the dough will be too dark and heavy. His original version also called for "massaged kale," which sounds a little precious, but Jonathan assured me (and my wife agrees, so who am I to argue?) that rubbing the kale leaves with lemon juice and salt helps break down the tough fibers, making the leaves easier to chew. I substitute baby kale for the full-grown leaves, so the "massaging" may not be necessary, but hey, it never hurts, and it may forever change your relationship with kale. After all, "Ben Essere" refers to the notion of well-being (*benessere*), a state of mind that Jonathan was able to evoke from this innovative yet true-to-the-spirit Neapolitan pizza.

Classic White Dough (page 26), made at least a day ahead, with the substitution of 1.5 ounces (43 grams) of coarse rye flour or other whole-grain flour to replace an equal amount of white flour, plus the addition of 2 tablespoons of sesame or hemp seeds

1 cup whole walnut pieces

¾ cup balsamic vinegar

3 young (small to medium size) beets

3 tablespoons olive oil

2 cups (packed) baby kale

2 tablespoons fresh lemon juice

½ teaspoon kosher salt

⅛ teaspoon black pepper

16 ounces (454 grams) fresh mozzarella (fior di latte)

8 ounces (227 grams) feta cheese

Three hours before making the pizzas, remove the dough from the refrigerator and divide it into 4 (9-ounce/255-gram) pieces, then form them into tight dough balls. Lightly mist a sheet pan or dough box with vegetable oil spray and place the dough balls on the pan or in the dough box. Mist the top of the dough balls with the oil spray and cover loosely with plastic wrap. Set aside at room temperature to proof for about 3 hours.

While the dough balls are rising, lightly toast the walnuts in a dry skillet over medium heat, slowly stirring for 4 to 6 minutes, until the nuts become too hot to touch and release a toasted, nutty aroma. Alternatively, bake them at 350°F on a dry sheet pan for 5 to 7 minutes. Transfer the nuts into a bowl and set aside.

While the nuts are cooling, bring the vinegar to a low boil in a saucepan over medium-high heat. Allow the volume to reduce to about half, until the vinegar thickens into a syrup. Remove the pan from the heat and set aside.

Wash and peel the beets. Use a mandoline or the thin slicing blade of a food processor to slice them paper-thin. Place them in a bowl and toss with 1 tablespoon of olive oil to coat. Set aside. In a separate bowl, combine the baby kale leaves, the remaining olive oil, the lemon juice and the salt and pepper. Gently massage the leaves with the salted lemon oil. Refrigerate.

When it's time to make the pizzas, place the baking stone or baking steel on the middle oven rack and preheat for 1 hour at 550°F, or as hot as the oven will allow. Dust a pizza peel with flour, semolina, or cornmeal, then stretch out a dough ball to a diameter of 12 inches (see page 18).

Cut or tear 4 ounces (113 grams) of fresh mozzarella per pizza into 9 or 10 small pieces and distribute them over the surface of the pizza, followed by one-fourth of the sliced beets, then one-fourth of the kale mixture. Slide the pizza into the oven and bake for about 4 minutes, then rotate and bake for an additional 2 to 3 minutes, until the crust turns golden brown on the rim (the cornicione) and on the underside.

Transfer the pizza to a cutting board and distribute 2 ounces (57 grams) of the feta cheese and one-fourth of the toasted walnuts over the surface. Slice and serve.

Peak Summer Corn Pie with Smoked Cheese

Makes 4 (12-inch) pizzas

Dan Richer is one of the biggest stars in the pizza universe. Razza, his pizzeria in Jersey City, New Jersey, is just a few minutes from Manhattan via car or the underground PATH train. Wait times are long, and the wood-fired sourdough pizzas are viewed with reverence by the lucky patrons who manage to get on the list. It's not just the seasonal, local ingredients, but also an attention to craft and detail found mainly at Michelin-starred restaurants that has created the aura of specialness around Razza. And Dan has been extremely generous in sharing his sourdough technique, as he demonstrated on a couple of episodes of *Pizza Talk*. He understands, as all the great ones do, that it's not the recipe that makes a pizza memorable, but the dedication and the hands of the one who is making it.

     This pizza, served only during the midsummer peak corn season, is a great example of simplicity elevated to true artisanship. The use of a small amount of *scamorza affumicata* (a smoked Southern Italian cheese in the same *pasta filata* cheese family as mozzarella but with a more robust flavor), plus the chili paste garnish, highlights the complex layering of flavor through the use of contrasting ingredients.

Sourdough Pizza Dough, made at least a day ahead (page 32), spiked with ¼ teaspoon instant yeast

1 teaspoon kosher or sea salt

4 ears summer fresh corn (will make about 2 cups kernels)

1 medium onion

16 ounces (454 grams) fresh mozzarella (*fior di latte*)

2 ounces (57 grams) smoked scamorza cheese or smoked mozzarella or smoked provolone

Freshly ground black pepper

Chili paste (such as Calabrian, sambal oelek, or other favorite variety)

Coarse or flake sea salt

4 teaspoons olive oil

Three hours before making the pizzas, remove the dough from the refrigerator and divide it into 4 (9-ounce/255-gram) pieces and form them into tight dough balls. Lightly mist a sheet pan or dough box with vegetable oil spray and place the dough balls on the pan or in the dough box. Mist the dough balls with the spray and cover loosely with plastic wrap. Set aside at room temperature to proof for about 3 hours.

While the dough is rising, bring 2 quarts of water to a boil, then add the salt and the corn. Simmer for 10 to 15 minutes. While corn is simmering, fill a large bowl with ice water. Transfer the corn to the ice water bath to stop the cooking. With a sharp knife, cut the kernels from the cob, place them in a bowl and set aside until assembly (if more than 3 hours ahead of baking the pizzas, cover and refrigerate the bowl of corn). Continue simmering the water.

Slice the onion into threads using a food processor with a slicing attachment, or slice thinly with a sharp knife. Drop the slices into the simmering pot of water and blanch for about 30 seconds. Use a skimmer or slotted spoon to remove and transfer the onions to a bowl, then let them cool at room temperature.

Cut the fresh mozzarella into 1-inch pieces, about the diameter of a quarter, and place the pieces in a bowl. Shred the smoked cheese and place it in its own bowl. Set the cheeses aside.

An hour before making the pizzas, place a baking stone or baking steel on the middle oven rack and preheat to 550°F, or as hot as the oven will allow.

Assemble the first pizza by stretching out a dough ball to 12 inches in diameter (see page 18). Lightly dust a pizza peel with flour, semolina, or cornmeal, then transfer the dough to the peel. Cover the surface of the dough with one-quarter of the corn kernels (about ½ cup). Distribute one-quarter of the fresh mozzarella cheese over the corn. Spread one-quarter of the blanched onion threads over the cheese, followed by one-quarter of the smoked cheese. Bake for 3 minutes, then rotate 180 degrees and continue baking for 2 to 4 minutes, until the crust is golden brown around the rim and on the underside, the cheese is caramelized on top, and the corn begins to char.

Transfer the pizza to a cutting board and drizzle a few drops of the chili paste over the surface, followed by 1 teaspoon of the olive oil. Garnish with a pinch of coarse or flake salt, to taste. Slice and serve.

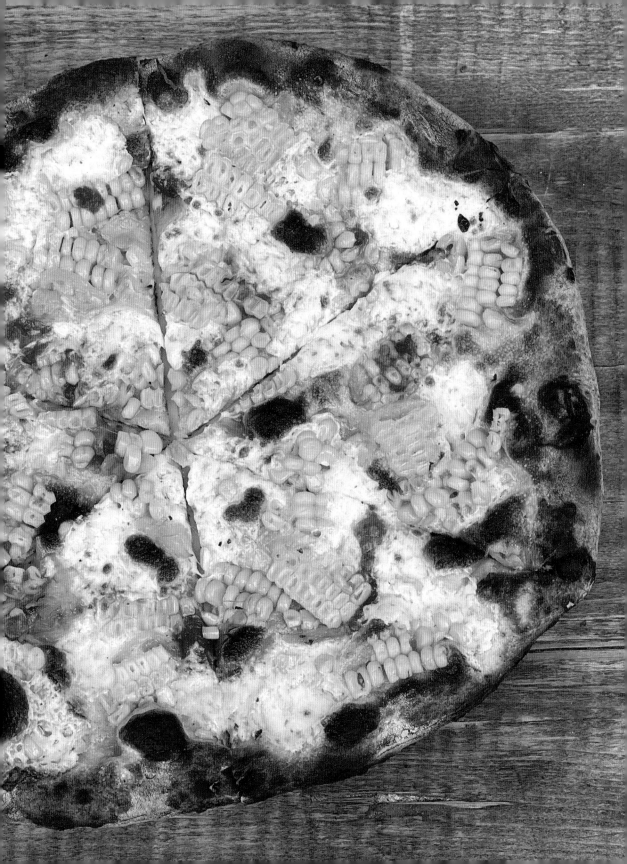

Nina Mae Levin

The Martha's Vineyard Corn and Shiitake Pie

Makes 4 (12-inch) pizzas

In one memorable episode of *Pizza Talk*, I interviewed Ed Levine, author of *Pizza: A Slice of Heaven* and founder of *Serious Eats*, the most influential food website of the past fifteen years. He was Zooming in from his summer home on Martha's Vineyard, which was fortuitous because the previous week, I had interviewed Glenn Roberts, another summer resident of Martha's Vineyard and the founder of Anson Mills, where the grains and seeds of the past are being reborn as the grains and seeds of the future.

When I asked both Glenn and Ed if there was any great pizza on the island, they each immediately began raving about a food truck called Stoney Hill Pizza and the woman at the helm, Nina Mae Levin. They implored me to come to the island as soon as possible and get one of Nina's corn and shiitake pizzas, as if it would be the next life-changing experience on my bucket list. If not for the pandemic, I would have immediately hopped on a plane; instead, I did the next best thing and contacted Nina and booked her for the show. We had a wonderful interview where I learned about her culinary journey, which included a stint in Charleston, SC, that inevitably led her to the Vineyard and, ultimately, to pizza (don't all such journeys end up at pizza?). Most importantly, she offered to share her Stoney Hill corn and shiitake pizza for this book.

In her description of the process, it was clear that a big part of the magic in her pizzas is the connection she has with her ingredients and suppliers, as well as with her dynamic, talented team. The transmission of love from the earth, through the hands of Nina and her crew, into every slice is palpable, in a manner very similar to what I saw with Dan Richer at Razza. It's no coincidence that both have made summer corn pizzas one of their signature items, but while not everyone can get Nina's Vineyard-grown Morning Glory Farm corn, or local MV Mycological mushrooms, or Maplebrook Farm fresh ricotta cheese—or products from any of the vendors she proudly shouts out on her menu—it's likely that many of us have access to our own local versions of such companies, which is really the point when we pay tribute to brilliant talent and artisanal products. So whether you grow it yourself or get it from your local farmer's market, or even from your local supermarkets, grab onto that sense of connectedness that Nina and all the pizzaiolos featured here embody.

At the end of our interview, I predicted that Martha's Vineyard would not be able to contain Nina's talent and energy forever, and I expect we will soon be hearing her name mentioned on a wider scale. Whatever the magic "it" is, Nina Mae Levin has it.

Sourdough Pizza Dough, made at least a day ahead (page 32) (Suggested option: Replace 10 percent of the bread flour with an equal amount of whole-wheat flour, sprouted whole-wheat flour, or heirloom whole-wheat flour—Nina uses Anson Mills Red Fife)

2 cups fresh corn kernels, preferably from locally grown corn (about 4 ears)

1 cup heavy cream

1 teaspoon coarse or flake sea salt (such as Maldon), divided

½ teaspoon freshly ground black pepper, divided

2 cups stemmed and sliced fresh shiitake mushrooms

¼ cup olive oil

2 cups ricotta cheese

2 teaspoons fresh oregano

1 cup freshly grated Parmesan cheese

Four hours before making the pizzas, remove the dough from the refrigerator and divide it into 4 (9-ounce/255-gram) pieces and form them into tight dough balls. Lightly mist a sheet pan or dough box with vegetable oil spray and place the dough balls on the pan or in the dough box. Mist the tops of the dough balls with vegetable oil spray, cover loosely with plastic wrap, and set aside at room temperature to proof for about 4 hours. If using sourdough that has been spiked with yeast (page 13), you can remove the dough 3 hours before baking instead of 4.

Combine the kernels and cream in a bowl. Add ½ teaspoon of salt (or to taste) and black pepper to taste. (Note: You can use frozen corn kernels or niblets, but they won't be quite as special.) Cover and refrigerate.

Preheat the oven to 550°F, or as hot as it will allow. In a bowl, toss together the sliced mushrooms and olive oil, sprinkle with ¼ teaspoon of the salt and ¼ teaspoon of the black pepper. Spread the mixture into a roasting pan or sheet pan and place it on the top rack of the preheated oven. Roast for 3 to 4 minutes, then turn on the broiler and cook an additional 2 to 3 minutes to fully dry and crisp the mushrooms. Remove the pan from the oven and set it aside so the mushrooms can cool. Assemble the remaining ingredients.

An hour before making the pizzas, place the baking stone or baking steel on the middle oven rack and preheat to 550°F, or as hot as the oven will allow. Prepare the first pizza by stretching out a dough ball (see page 18) to a diameter of 12 inches. Lightly dust a pizza peel with flour, semolina, or cornmeal, then transfer the dough to the peel. Cover the surface of the dough with one-quarter of the corn and cream mixture, leaving an uncovered border of ½ inch around the perimeter. Distribute one-quarter of the roasted shiitakes over the corn. Use ½ cup of ricotta cheese per pizza and, with a teaspoon, scoop and drop evenly spaced dollops of it over the surface of the pizza. Slide the pizza into the oven and bake for 3 minutes, then rotate 180 degrees and continue baking an additional 2 to 4 minutes, until the crust is golden brown around the edge and on the underside.

Transfer the pizza to a cutting board and sprinkle
½ teaspoon of oregano and ¼ cup of Parmesan
over the surface. Sprinkle on salt and pepper
to taste. Slice and serve while preparing the
next pizza.

Mike Kurtz

The Hellboy Slice Pizza

Makes 3 (14-inch) pizzas

Here's the history of this pizza from Mike Kurtz himself:

The Hellboy was born out of Paulie Gee's pizzeria in Greenpoint, Brooklyn. I was a pizza hobbyist in 2010, working in the music business, but had been making honey, infused with chili peppers, as a hobby for about six years at that point. I met Paulie Gee when he first opened his wood-fired pizzeria in Greenpoint, and he invited me to become a pizza apprentice there. After my day job in Manhattan, I'd go into the pizzeria at night to practice stretching dough. Once I was fast enough, Paulie started scheduling me for dinner shifts.

One day I brought in a bottle of my hot honey for Paulie to try on his pizza. It was always called Mike's Hot Honey from day one, but was unbranded at the time. Paulie liked it on his soppressata pie and asked if I could make enough for the restaurant to add it to the menu. The original pie that featured the hot honey was called "Fire Up the Delboy." Delboy (a nickname for Paulie's son Derek) was a pie with, as we say, tomatoes, "fresh mootz," parm, and soppressata picante from Salumeria Biellese. This was Derek's favorite pie. When the expeditors at the pizzeria would call out a pie to be made, they would say, "Fire up the Delboy!" So when we added Mike's Hot Honey to the Delboy, we initially named the pie "Fire Up the Delboy." That was a mouthful, and when one of the customers suggested "Hellboy" instead, we ran with it.

When Paulie later opened Paulie Gee's Slice Shop, he made a New York Thin Crust variation of The Hellboy featuring tomatoes, Grande mozzarella, Ezzo (cup and char style) pepperoni, and a post-oven drizzle of Mike's Hot Honey.

Postscript: And, as the saying goes, the rest was history, and now Mike's Hot Honey is found all over the world. The key to its use, as Mike told me when I interviewed him on *Pizza Talk*, is to always drizzle on the hot honey post-oven, after cutting the pie and just before eating: "You want to drizzle and then eat it right away." I don't think that last suggestion about eating it right away is really necessary. Do you?

New York Pizza Dough (page 30)

Crushed Tomato Pizza Sauce (page 42)

16 ounces (454 grams) shredded low-moisture mozzarella cheese, full fat or half low fat (about 4 cups)

2 cups sliced cup and char pepperoni, or spicy soppressata or other favorite salumi

1 cup freshly grated Parmesan cheese

6 ounces (170 grams or 1 cup) Mike's Hot Honey or substitute*

*Hot Honey, page 67

Three hours before making the pizzas, remove the dough from the refrigerator and divide it into 3 (12-ounce/340-gram) pieces. Lightly mist a sheet pan or dough box with vegetable oil spray. Form the dough pieces into tight dough balls and place them on the pan or in the dough box. Mist the top of the dough balls with the oil spray and loosely cover the pan with plastic wrap. Set the dough aside at room temperature to proof for about 3 hours.

While the dough is rising, prepare the sauce and assemble the other ingredients.

An hour before making the pizzas, place a baking stone or baking steel on the middle oven rack and preheat to 550°F or as hot as the oven will allow.

Assemble the first pizza by stretching out a dough ball (see page 18). Lightly dust a pizza peel with flour, semolina, or cornmeal, then transfer the dough to the peel. Cover the surface of the dough with ½ cup of the sauce, leaving a rim about ½ inch around the edge uncovered. Distribute one-third of the mozzarella (about 1⅓ cups) over the sauce, followed by one-third of the pepperoni (about ⅔ cup). Bake for 3 minutes, then rotate 180 degrees and continue baking for an additional 2 to 4 minutes, until the crust is golden brown around the edge and on the underside, the cheese is golden, and the pepperoni is curled and charred.

Transfer the pizza to a cutting board and distribute ⅓ cup of the Parmesan over the surface. Then drizzle about 3 tablespoons of the hot honey, streaking it over the surface of the pizza. Slice and serve.

Mark and Jenny Bello

The Hot Honion

Makes 4 (12-inch) pizzas

It doesn't get much simpler than this—but this pizza is brilliant in its simplicity. Mark and Jenny Bello own and operate Pizza School NYC in Manhattan, where they have taught more than 50,000 students over the past ten years how to make killer pizzas for both home and professional use. During that time, they've met and befriended a lot of talented people and learned a few tricks that they then pass on to others. One of their close friends is Mike Kurtz, founder of Mike's Hot Honey, which the Bellos watched grow from a clever idea into a juggernaut commercial product. The hot honey is one of the keys to bringing this onion pizza to life, as is another "secret" ingredient that Mark loves: crispy onions. He recommends the Lars Own brand, which may be hard to find other than online, so I've included an easy hack that enables you to make your own version of this wonderful condiment. The synergy between the soft onions and the hot honey, along with the crunch factor provided by the crispy onions and the crust, delivers a flavor and texture satisfaction equal to the much more complexly topped pizzas we usually make or eat.

Classic White Dough (page 26), made at least a day ahead

1 large or 2 medium red onions, sliced paper thin (about 4 cups, loosely packed)

4 ounces (113 grams) whole milk mozzarella, provolone, fontina or other good-melting cheese, shredded

4 ounces (113 grams) part-skim milk (low-fat) mozzarella, shredded

4 tablespoons Mike's Hot Honey, or your own homemade version (recipe follows)

½ cup crispy onions, such as Lars Own brand (available online, or make your own; recipe follows)

Three hours before baking the pizza, remove the dough from the refrigerator and divide it into 4 (9-ounce/255-gram) pieces. Lightly mist a sheet pan or dough box with vegetable oil spray. Form the dough pieces into tight dough balls and place them on the pan or in the dough box. Mist the tops of the dough balls with the oil spray and cover the pan loosely with plastic wrap. Set it aside to proof at room temperature for about 3 hours.

While the dough is proofing, prepare the toppings.

An hour before making the pizzas, place a baking stone or baking steel on the middle oven rack and preheat to 550°F or as hot as the oven will allow. Lightly dust a pizza peel with flour, semolina, or cornmeal, then transfer the dough to the peel.

When you're ready to bake, assemble the first pizza by stretching out a dough ball to 12 inches in diameter (see page 18). Distribute one-quarter of each type of shredded cheese (about 1 cup total) over the surface, leaving a ½-inch border around the perimeter without cheese. Distribute about 1 cup of the sliced onions over the cheese. Slide the pizza onto the baking stone or steel and bake for 3 minutes, then rotate 180 degrees and continue baking for 2 to 4 minutes, until the crust is golden brown around the edge and on the underside.

Transfer the pizza to a cutting board and drizzle 1 tablespoon of the hot honey (or to taste) over the surface. Sprinkle 1 to 2 tablespoons of the crispy onions over the pizza, then slice and serve.

Hot Honey

½ cup honey

Cayenne powder

Place honey in a saucepan and heat to lukewarm. Whisk in ¼ to ½ teaspoon cayenne, to taste. Set aside at room temperature.

Crispy Onions

1 cup vegetable oil

½ cup dried onions (from supermarket spice section)

In a saucepan, heat the oil to 350°F. Line a plate with a paper towel. With a skimmer or slotted spoon, stir in the onions, which will crisp and brown up in less than a minute. Transfer the onions to the plate. (You can make more batches for later use, as the onions will be useable for up to two weeks if kept in an airtight container.)

The Monte Cristo

Makes 4 (12-inch) pizzas

The Paulie Gee story is a phenomenon. Paul Giannone had already had a thirty-year career as a corporate IT executive when he decided, as the saying goes, enough is enough. He followed his bliss, opened a wood-fired pizzeria in Greenpoint, Brooklyn, in 2010, and, in a very short time, became known to the world as "the legendary Paulie Gee." What makes him legendary, aside from the amazing pizzas and the rapid opening of other branches as far away as Chicago (see page 117 for a pizza from Derrick Tung's Logan Square branch), is that he immediately became a mentor and role model to a whole crew of talented pizza newbies, and Paulie Gee's in Greenpoint turned into the mother house for the next generation of talent. Paulie and his wife, Maryann, embody the virtues and principles they espouse and transmit to their employees and customers: hospitality and welcomeness, kindness, a willingness to share knowledge, and, of course, amazing pizzas with whimsical names. As a result, The Hellboy, Ricky Ricotta, Cherry Jones, Sake Mountain Way, Ricotta Be Kiddin' Me, and many more pizzas have become destination pies for both locals and pizza pilgrims. And did I already mention he's become legendary in less than ten years?!

Here's a tribute version of one of Paulie's favorites, The Monte Cristo. It's simple yet elegant, and when I suggested to Paulie the addition of a baked egg on top and he responded, "No, it's already perfect and doesn't need a friggin' egg on top—it's the maple syrup that ties it all together!" you know he's right.

Classic White Dough (page 26) or Sourdough Pizza Dough (with yeast added, page 32), made at least a day ahead

20 ounces (567 grams) mild Gouda cheese (or fontina, cheddar, or gruyere, or a combination, though Paulie uses only Gouda), shredded (about 6 cups)

8 ounces (227 grams) Canadian bacon or Black Forest ham, sliced ¼ inch thick and cut into discs 2 inches in diameter, or cut into wedges if the diameter is larger than 2 inches

½ cup maple syrup

Three hours before baking, remove the dough from the refrigerator. Divide and shape 4 dough balls of 9 ounces (255 grams) each. Mist a sheet pan with vegetable or olive oil spray and place the dough balls on the pan. Mist the tops lightly with the spray and cover the pan loosely with plastic wrap. Set aside to proof at room temperature for about 3 hours. Meanwhile, prepare the other ingredients and keep them refrigerated until assembly.

An hour before making the pizzas, place a baking stone or baking steel on the middle oven rack and preheat to 550°F or as hot as the oven will allow.

When it's time to bake, begin stretching the dough balls (see page 18) to 12 inches in diameter. Assemble 1 pizza at a time, preparing the next pizza while the previous one is baking. Lightly dust a pizza peel with flour, semolina, or cornmeal, then transfer the dough to the peel. Cover the surface with 1½ cups of the shredded Gouda, leaving an uncovered border about ½ inch wide around the edge. Evenly space 8 slices of the Canadian bacon or ham on top of the cheese. Warm the maple syrup in a small saucepan on low heat, to about 120°F.

Slide the pizza onto the baking stone and bake for 4 minutes, then rotate and bake for 2 to 4 minutes longer, until the cheese is bubbly and beginning to caramelize, the edge (cornicione) is puffy and golden brown, and the underside is also golden brown.

Transfer the pizza to a cutting board. Drizzle about 2 tablespoons of the warm maple syrup in streaks over the pizza. Slice and serve.

Lox and Cream Cheese Pizza on Chicken Schmaltz Crust

Makes 3 (14-inch) pizzas

Noel Brohner wears many hats from his home base in Los Angeles. He's a concert and events producer, a private chef, a major Instagram presence (@Slowrisepizza), and an international pizza consultant. When the 2020 International Pizza Expo was canceled due to the pandemic, Noel organized a weeklong Zoom-based pizza party to bring the speakers, pizza operators, and vendors together and fill the void caused by this major disruption in everyone's lives. This gathering inspired my idea for *Pizza Talk,* which launched a couple of months after Noel's virtual pizza party, because I just wanted to keep the conversation going.

One of the many innovative pizzas Noel has created over the years is a lox and bagel pizza favored by some of his private clients, many of whom are major players in the Hollywood film scene. This pizza was first popularized about 35 years ago by the late great pizza genius at Wolfgang Puck's Spago, Ed LaDou, but Noel's version takes it to another level with the use of chicken fat (schmaltz) in place of olive oil in the dough, along with some clever garnishes.

The interconnected relationship between sandwiches and pizza has, for a long time, been responsible for the never-ending topping concepts that roll out every year around the pizza world. For those of us who, like myself, grew up with lox and bagel sandwiches as a regular Sunday or special occasion food, it's perfectly logical—a no-brainer, really—that this concept is perfect for pizza. My tribute version of Noel's masterpiece translates his push-the-envelope creativity into a very doable version for anyone, whether for Sundays, special occasions, or just anytime you start craving one of the great flavor combinations in the culinary canon.

Note: Unlike most of the pizzas in this book, the dough for this one is rolled out instead of hand-stretched. The purpose is to produce a thinner crust and to extend it into a wider diameter than for Neapolitan pizzas. This will produce a chewier, more bagel-like texture.

New York Pizza Dough (page 30) made at least a day ahead, with the option to replace the olive oil with an equal amount of chicken schmaltz (recipe follows)

1 quart of cherry or grape tomatoes, halved

1 teaspoon kosher or coarse sea salt

Large red onion, julienned

½ cup red wine vinegar or apple cider vinegar

¼ cup olive oil or chicken fat (schmaltz)

2 tablespoons capers

3 shallots, sliced into strips, or crispy onions, such as Lars Own or homemade (page 68)

8 ounces (227 grams) cream cheese, fresh goat cheese, or crème fraîche

2 tablespoons sour cream, milk, cream, or yogurt

1 English or Persian cucumber

2 tablespoons Everything Bagel Topping (combine all ingredients and adjust to taste)

- 1 tablespoon sesame seeds
- 1 tablespoon poppy seeds
- 1 teaspoon granulated or dried garlic flakes
- 1 teaspoon dried onion bits
- ¼ to ½ teaspoon kosher, coarse, or flake salt

8 ounces (227 grams) thinly sliced smoked salmon (lox)

2 tablespoons lemon juice

2 or 3 sprigs fresh dill, chopped

3 chives, diced

1 teaspoon freshly grated lemon zest

1 organic lemon, sliced into 6 wedges

Three hours before baking the pizzas, remove the dough from the refrigerator and divide it into 3 (12-ounce/340-gram) pieces. Lightly mist a sheet pan or dough box with vegetable oil spray. Form the dough pieces into tight dough balls and place them on the pan or in the dough box. Mist the dough with the spray and loosely cover the pan with plastic wrap. Set aside at room temperature to proof for about 3 hours.

While the dough is proofing, preheat the oven to 350°F. Lay out the tomatoes on a sheet pan, sprinkle them lightly with salt, and roast for 15 minutes. Turn off the oven and let the tomatoes continue to dry out as the oven cools. While the tomatoes are roasting and drying, place the julienned onion slices in a bowl. Bring the vinegar to a boil and pour it over the onions, stirring to coat. Set the onions aside to cool.

In a small saucepan, heat the olive oil or schmaltz until it shimmers, stir in the capers, and fry for 2 to 3 minutes, until they swell. Strain the capers from the oil, place them in a small bowl, and set aside to cool. Bring the fat back to a shimmer over high heat and stir in the shallots. Cook for 3 to 5 minutes, until the shallots begin to char on the outside. Drain the shallots from the oil and place them in a bowl to cool. Set aside the pan of oil to cool.

In a separate bowl, whisk the cream cheese, fresh goat cheese or crème fraîche with the sour cream, milk, cream, or yogurt until it is soft and fluffy (you can also use the whisk attachment of a stand mixer). Cover and refrigerate. Using a mandoline, ceramic vegetable slicer, or sharp knife, peel and slice the cucumber as thinly as possible, then place in a bowl, cover, and refrigerate.

An hour before making the pizzas, place a baking stone or baking steel on the middle oven rack and preheat to 550°F or as hot as the oven will allow. Begin rolling out the dough by dusting the work surface with flour and flattening one dough ball at a time with your palm. Flip the dough over so both sides are dusted with flour, then begin rolling out one dough at a time with a rolling pin, working from the center to the outer perimeter in all directions. Continue dusting with flour, as needed, to prevent sticking, and roll out the dough into a circle with a diameter of 14 inches.

Lightly dust a pizza peel with flour, cornmeal, or semolina. Transfer the first dough that's ready to the peel, then use a fork to dock the surface of the dough with holes all over to minimize ballooning in the oven. Check to see that the dough still slides on the peel, then brush some of the oil or schmaltz from frying the capers and shallots over the surface. Sprinkle about 2 teaspoons of the bagel topping over the dough.

Slide the dough onto the hot baking stone and bake for 3 minutes, then rotate 180 degrees and continue baking for an additional 1 to 3 minutes, until the dough bubbles and is golden brown on the top and the underside. Transfer it to a cooling rack or cutting board and bake the other doughs in the same manner.

When it's time to assemble the pizzas, return the baked crusts, one at a time, to the oven for about 1 minute to reheat, and then cover the surface with the sliced cucumbers. Distribute the pickled onions over the cucumbers, followed by the slices of smoked salmon (lox). Drizzle 1 or 2 teaspoons of fresh lemon juice over the salmon, then distribute one-third of the tomatoes over the lox. Pipe or drop dollops of the whipped cream cheese or goat cheese over the pizza, evenly spaced, and garnish with the fried capers, charred shallots, some springs of fresh dill, and a sprinkling of lemon zest. Slice into wedges or squares and serve with 2 wedges of lemon while assembling the next pizza.

Note: You can freeze any unused baked pizza crusts for later use, reheating them in a 400°F oven for 3 to 5 minutes just before serving.

Chicken Schmaltz

There are many methods for rendering chicken fat. The easiest is to simmer a whole chicken or cut chicken parts in water for about an hour, then cool and save the broth in plastic containers overnight in the refrigerator. The next day, collect the congealed fat (schmaltz) that has formed on top of the broth with a spoon, and keep it in a separate container. However, what I often do is collect rendered fat from the pan when I roast or bake a whole chicken or chicken pieces, the same as when cooking bacon. The difference is that the fat will be seasoned by whatever spices I rubbed on the chicken, but that just makes the schmaltz even more interesting. Once the fat is collected and chilled, you can use it like butter or ghee. It will keep for at least 3 weeks in the refrigerator.

Will Grant

The Caputo Cup Championship White Sourdough Pizza

Makes 2 (16-inch) pizzas

Will Grant, owner of That's A'Some Pizza on Bainbridge Island, across Puget Sound from Seattle, Washington, was unknown to most of the pizza world until he won the Caputo Cup championship in 2017 in Atlantic City. Despite years in the restaurant business, he had only just completed a pizza course at Tony Gemignani's International School of Pizza, and it was Tony who suggested entering the competition. So, using his family's heirloom sourdough starter, Will entered a simple white pie that blew the judges away and was declared the winner in the Non-Traditional category. I remember that pizza because I was one of those judges, and it caught us all by surprise. The rest is history, as Tony then invited Will to join the World Pizza Champions Team, and business at the pizzeria grew enough for Will to open a second place, Sourdough Willy's Pizzeria, on the Kitsap Peninsula in Kingston, Washington, where he again deploys his 120-year-old starter—which, by the way, is registered and repeatedly refreshed at the Puratos Sourdough Library in St. Vith, Belgium (number 104 in their catalogue)—to make Sicilian, Roman, and Detroit-style pies. In just the few years since Will's victorious run began, he has become, like Dan Richer, Anthony Mangieri, and Sarah Minnick, among others, one of the true ambassadors of this important sourdough fermentation trend.

Here is my tribute version of Will's Caputo Cup winner. The topping combination is nicely inventive, but it's not a complicated pie once you have the sourdough crust nailed down, so this one really highlights how much a great crust can elevate a pie when properly crafted.

Sourdough Pizza Dough (page 32, "purist version," made at least a day ahead)

Gorgonzola creme (recipe follows; make a day ahead if making your own crème fraîche)

5 ounces (142 grams) whole milk mozzarella, shredded

5 ounces (142 grams) provolone cheese, shredded

2 pints button or cremini mushrooms

1 large red onion

1 head garlic, peeled and minced

1 cup crumbled feta cheese

Four hours before baking, remove the dough from the refrigerator and divide it into 2 (18-ounce/510-gram) pieces. Lightly mist a sheet pan or dough box with vegetable oil spray. Form the dough pieces into tight dough balls and place them on the pan or in the dough box. Mist the top of the dough balls with the spray and cover loosely with plastic wrap. Set the pan aside to proof at room temperature for about 4 hours.

Make the Gorgonzola creme (recipe follows). Combine the shredded mozzarella and provolone in one bowl. Wipe and stem the whole mushrooms with a wet paper towel and thinly slice them to about ⅛ inch wide, discarding the stems if they are woody, or using them if they are soft. Set aside. Julienne the onion into thin strips and set the slices aside.

An hour before making the pizzas, place a baking stone or baking steel on the middle oven rack and preheat to 550°F or as hot as the oven will allow. When it's time to make the pizzas,

lightly dust the work surface with flour and begin stretching the first dough (see page 18), resting it as needed if the dough resists or begins shrinking back. The opened dough should be about 16 inches in diameter. Lightly dust a pizza peel with flour, cornmeal, or semolina and lay the shaped dough on it, making sure it slides easily. Cover the surface with half of the cheese blend, leaving a border of ½ inch around the perimeter without cheese. Distribute half of the mushrooms over the cheese, followed by half of the onions. Drizzle half of the Gorgonzola creme over the surface, followed by half of the garlic.

Bake the pizza for 4 minutes, then rotate 180 degrees and continue baking for an additional 3 to 5 minutes, until the cheese is bubbly and golden, and the crust is golden brown around the edge and on the underside. Transfer the pizza to a cutting board and distribute half of the feta cheese over the surface. Slice and serve.

Gorgonzola Creme

4 ounces (113 grams) firm Gorgonzola cheese or another blue cheese, such as Danish

4 ounces (113 grams) crème fraîche or sour cream

1 teaspoon dried chives or 2 fresh chives, coarsely chopped

2 cloves fresh garlic, pressed or chopped, or ½ teaspoon granulated garlic

½ teaspoon kosher salt

¼ teaspoon ground black pepper

Place all ingredients—Gorgonzola cheese, crème fraîche, chives, garlic, salt, and pepper—in a blender or food processor and process until smooth. Add more crème fraîche or sour cream if you want a milder blue cheese flavor.

Sarah Minnick

Summer Peach and Corn Pizza

Makes 4 (12-inch) pizzas

Sarah Minnick has carved out a nice slice of heaven for herself and her family in Northeast Portland, Oregon, where she crafts beautiful farm-to-fork naturally fermented sourdough (made with a starter named Jake) pizzas, with ample edible flowers, and—hooray—also makes her own ice cream at her (and her sister Jane's) restaurant, Lovely's Fifty Fifty (the name refers to fifty percent pizzas and fifty percent ice cream). The beauty of her work is clearly evident on the restaurant website and social media postings.

The menu features only a few pizza choices each day, determined by whatever is fresh and at peak that day from Sarah's posse of local growers and ingredient providers. During the summer, more and more pizzerias, such as Tony Gemignani's with its peach-centric creation (page 80), cannot resist using tree-ripened fruit and finding ways to pair it with savory ingredients. Here's our tribute version of one of Sarah's most well-known destination summer pizzas, paired with fresh corn (summer corn is a major motif in this book, it would seem) and pancetta. I admit, just seeing those words—peaches, corn, pancetta—in the same sentence makes me crave one right now!

Sourdough Pizza Dough (page 32, "purist" or "spiked" version), made at least a day ahead

4 large or 6 medium ripe peaches (tree ripened if possible)

2 large or 3 small ears fresh corn

2 cups chopped frisée or baby arugula

6 ounces (170 grams) pancetta (optional)

8 ounces (227 grams) shredded whole milk mozzarella (about 2 cups)

8 ounces (227 grams) shredded fontina cheese (about 2 cups)

4 teaspoons fresh summer savory, or 2 teaspoons dried

Remove the dough from the refrigerator 4 hours before baking if using the "purist" dough; 3 hours before for the "spiked" dough. Divide it into 4 (9-ounce/255-gram) pieces. Lightly mist a sheet pan or dough box with vegetable oil spray. Form the dough pieces into tight dough balls and place them on the pan or in the dough box. Mist the dough balls with the spray and cover loosely with plastic wrap. Set aside to proof at room temperature for 3 or 4 hours, depending on whether you're using the spiked or purist version.

While the dough is proofing, bring a 2-quart pot of water to a boil. Prepare a bowl of ice water and set aside. Gently drop each of the peaches into the boiling water and simmer for 2 to 4 minutes, until the skins soften and separate from the fruit (the riper the fruit, the shorter the simmering time). Transfer them with a slotted spoon into the ice water for 2 minutes to stop the cooking (leave the hot water simmering for the corn).

Carefully peel off and discard the peach skins, then halve the peaches to dig out the pits. Cut each half into four equal-size wedges, leaving you with 8 sections for each pizza (if using smaller peaches, cut into 6 wedges each). Place the peach sections in a covered bowl and refrigerate. Place the ears of corn into the hot water and simmer for about 10 minutes, until the kernels become tender. Use a pair of tongs to transfer the corn into the ice water to stop the cooking, then use a sharp knife to slice the kernels from the cob. Collect the kernels and place them in a bowl. Cover and refrigerate.

Gather the remaining ingredients, washing and drying the frisée. Chop the frisée into bite-size pieces, place in a bowl, and refrigerate. If using pancetta, slice it into 1-inch-long slivers, about ½ inch wide. Cook it over medium-high heat in a frying pan or skillet for 3 to 5 minutes, stirring to render off some of the fat, until cooked but not crisp. With a slotted spoon or tongs, collect the pancetta from the rendered fat and set it aside in a bowl. Discard the fat, or save it for future use (including as a substitute for oil in dough). Combine both types of shredded cheese in a single bowl.

An hour before making the pizzas, place a baking stone or baking steel on the middle oven rack and preheat to 550°F or as hot as the oven will allow.

Lightly dust a pizza peel with flour, semolina, or cornmeal. Stretch out a dough ball (see page 18). Distribute 1 cup of the cheese blend over the surface, leaving a ½-inch border around the perimeter without cheese. Distribute ½ cup of the frisee over the cheese, then evenly lay out 8 peach slices over the greens, followed by a sprinkling of one-quarter of the corn kernels. If using pancetta slivers, distribute one-quarter of them over the surface.

Slide the pizza into the oven and bake for about 3 minutes, then rotate 180 degrees and bake for an additional 2 to 4 minutes, until the crust turns golden brown around the edge (cornicione) and on the underside.

Transfer the pizza to a cutting board and garnish with 1 teaspoon of the fresh summer savory (½ teaspoon if using dried savory). Slice and serve.

Peaches and Cream California-Style Pizza

Makes 4 (12-inch) pizzas

The name Tony Gemignani appears often throughout these pages, not only for the two pizzas of his that are featured but because he has been such a major influence on many of the other pizza stars also featured. He is the most decorated pizzaiolo in America, if not the world, not only for his award-winning pizzas and restaurants, but also for his work as a practically unbeatable acrobatic dough-tossing competitor and founder of the World Pizza Champions Team, and for Tony Gemignani's International School of Pizza (part of the international Scuola Italiana Pizzaioli), where he trains the next generation of pizza stars. In my video interviews with Tony, I often refer to him as the "Mozart of pizza" because he is adept at every style and, like Mozart, is unquenchably prolific. I've known Tony for many years, before all the awards came pouring in and before he became the reigning rock star of the pizza universe, and have interviewed him many times. I've really enjoyed watching him grow and mature into an authentic mentor, totally committed to his craft and generous beyond measure.

Here's an example of a pizza you may not find at his restaurants, with Tony's description of the reason he gave me permission to include it in this book:

This pizza reminds me of one of the first times we met in person, and it was at the Ferry Terminal Market in San Francisco, where we ate the most amazing, juice-dripping-down-our-chins Frog Hollow Farm peaches. Whenever I make this pizza I remember us literally salivating over those peaches.

I, too, remember that meeting and those peaches, perhaps the finest peaches I've ever eaten. Food memories like that are indelible, so I'm glad to hear it was as memorable for Tony as it was for me.

The following pizza has its origins even earlier, when Tony and Chef Courtney Townsend won The Franciscan Estates Pizza Battle in Napa, against two much more famous (at the time) restaurant chefs from high-profile restaurants. Tony and Courtney had to make 15 of these pizzas, along with an equal number of a second pizza (one that was built around duck confit — I'd love to get my hands on that recipe!). Taking home that crown during the earlier days of his career has kept this pizza as one of Tony's personal favorites.

Note: This recipe calls for Gorgonzola dolce, a softer, creamier, milder version of the famous Italian blue cheese. It is not crumbly, but soft enough to scoop from its rind (almost like a ripe Brie or Camembert) and is used in many sauces, such as the Gorgonzola Dolce Cream that Tony makes for this pizza. You should be able to find this cheese at specialty cheese shops, or ask the cheese buyer at your local supermarket.

Classic White Dough, Neapolitan variation (page 26), made at least a day ahead

16 ounces (454 grams) shredded whole milk mozzarella (about 4 cups, packed)

2 cups walnut halves

1½ cups granulated sugar, divided

¾ cup water, divided

6 ounces (170 grams) Gorgonzola dolce

½ cup whipping cream

½ cup balsamic vinegar

4 large (or 6 small) ripe peaches (freestone if possible)

Coarse or flaky sea salt (such as Maldon)

Three hours before making the pizzas, remove the dough from the refrigerator and divide it into 4 pieces weighing 9 ounces (255 grams) each. Lightly mist a sheet pan or dough box with vegetable oil spray. Form the dough pieces into dough balls and place them on the pan or in the dough box. Mist the top of the dough balls with the oil spray and cover loosely with plastic wrap. Set the dough aside at room temperature to proof for about 3 hours.

While the dough is rising, prepare the candied walnuts by combining the walnut pieces, 1 cup of the sugar, and ¼ cup water in a saucepan and bringing the water to a boil. Line a sheet pan with a silicone baking mat or a baking parchment misted lightly with vegetable oil spray. When the water mixture comes to a boil, gently stir the walnuts in the sugar syrup until the syrup reduces to a clear, thick coating, about the consistency of honey. Do not bring the syrup to a caramel color. Pour the mixture onto the prepared pan, separate the walnuts with a wooden spoon and set the pan aside to let the candied walnuts cool and harden.

To make the Gorgonzola dolce cream, use an electric mixer fitted with the paddle attachment or whisk by hand in a bowl. Place the gorgonzola dolce into the bowl and mix in the cream, beating on medium speed, or whisking, until the cheese disappears into the cream and forms a smooth, stiff mixture. Cover the bowl and refrigerate.

An hour before making the pizzas, place a baking stone or baking steel on the middle oven rack and preheat to 550°F or as hot as the oven will allow. While the oven is preheating, bring the balsamic vinegar to a simmer in a saucepan and cook it over medium heat until it reduces by half and thickens into a honey-like syrup. Remove the pan from the heat and set it aside.

In a separate saucepan, make a simple syrup by combining the remaining sugar and water and bringing it to a boil. Simmer for about 4 minutes, or until it reduces slightly, then turn off the heat. While the syrup is cooling, slice each of the peaches, skin on, into 8 wedges (6 if using small peaches), removing the pit and any slivers of the seed. Lay the slices out on a sheet pan and brush them on both sides with the hot simple syrup.

Stretch out a dough ball (see page 18). Lightly dust a pizza peel with flour, semolina, or cornmeal, then transfer the dough to the peel. Cover the surface of the dough with one-quarter of the mozzarella (about 1 cup), leaving a rim of about ½ inch around the edge uncovered. Bake the pizza for 3 minutes, then rotate 180 degrees and continue baking for 2 to 4 minutes, until the crust is golden brown around the edge (cornicione) and on the underside, and the cheese is melted and beginning to lightly caramelize.

Transfer the pizza to a cutting board and distribute one-fourth of the candied walnuts over the surface of the hot cheese. Lay out 6 (or 8) peach wedges evenly around the pie, followed by 7 (or 9) dollops of the Gorgonzola dolce cream between the peaches, including one in the center of the pizza. Drizzle the balsamic syrup in a spiral (or in streaks) over the surface of the pizza. Sprinkle a pinch of the salt over the top. Slice and serve.

Grant Arons

Pistachio Pesto Neapolitan Pizza

Makes 4 (12-inch) pizzas

Grant Arons has, for many years, successfully operated what I call a "college–style" pizzeria, Farley's Pizzeria, near the University of North Carolina at Charlotte. But when he saw what was happening in the world of wood-fired Neapolitan pizza—and experienced for himself the pizzas of Naples—he felt an overwhelming, almost obsessive urge to go all-in and to learn everything he could about it. His journey eventually manifested as Inizio Pizza Napoletana, also right here in Charlotte, about three miles from where I live, and we soon got to know each other. Inizio is modeled on the successful Antico Pizza Napoletana in Atlanta. Like at Antico, long, family-style tables found (pre-COVID, at least) strangers dining beside strangers in a congenial, community-like fashion, eating gorgeous Inizio pizzas, both classic Napoletana as well as some in-house creations, such as his Pistachio Pesto Neapolitan Pizza, which has become a local favorite and Inizio's signature pizza.

Here's Grant's description:

This pizza is based on the traditional use of pistachio in the Neapolitan food culture. We wanted a beautiful, eye-catching, and delicious creation that you couldn't find anywhere else. The green color of the pizza, with melty Buffalo mozzarella and dollops of rich ricotta, set the tone for decadence without any heavy meats. The aroma of fresh rosemary and pistachio really sets this pizza up as something special. It has become Inizio Pizza Napoletana's cult favorite and it's the pizza we get the most compliments on.

And so, here is my tribute version of Inizio's cult favorite.

Classic White Dough (page 26), made at least a day ahead

Pistachio Pesto (recipe follows)

8 ounces (227 grams) ricotta cheese

2 ounces (57 grams) heavy cream

8 ounces (227 grams) whole milk mozzarella, shredded (about 2 cups)

8 ounces (227 grams) mozzarella di bufala or fior di latte, cut into 16 pieces

4 teaspoons fresh rosemary needles

1 cup unsalted shelled pistachios, lightly toasted (for garnish)

½ cup grated Pecorino Romano or Parmesan

Three hours before baking, remove the dough from the refrigerator and divide it into 4 (9-ounce/255-gram) pieces. Lightly mist a sheet pan or dough box with vegetable oil spray. Form the dough pieces into tight dough balls and place them on the pan or in the dough box. Mist the tops lightly with the spray and cover the pan loosely with plastic wrap. Set aside at room temperature to proof for about 3 hours.

While the dough is proofing, prepare the pesto (recipe follows) or bring the already prepared pesto to room temperature. Whisk together the ricotta and cream, or puree it in the blender, to form a smooth sauce. Set aside.

An hour before making the pizzas, place a baking stone or baking steel on the middle oven rack and preheat to 550°F or as hot as the oven will allow. When it's time to bake the pizzas, begin stretching the dough ball (see page 18) to about 12 inches in diameter. Assemble 1 pizza at a time, preparing the next while the previous one is baking.

Lightly dust a pizza peel with flour, semolina, or cornmeal, then transfer the dough to the peel. Cover the surface of the dough with about ¾ cup of the pesto, leaving a border around the perimeter of about ½ inches without sauce. Evenly distribute ½ cup of the shredded mozzarella over the surface, followed by 4 evenly spaced pieces of the fresh mozzarella. Put dollops of the ricotta cream in between the fresh mozzarella pieces. Sprinkle 1 teaspoon of the rosemary needles over the top,

Slide the pizza into the oven and bake for about 3 minutes, then rotate 180 degrees and continue baking for 2 to 4 minutes, until the edge (cornicione) of the crust is puffy and golden brown, and the underside is also golden brown. Transfer the pizza onto a cutting board and garnish with ¼ cup of the pistachio nuts and 2 tablespoons of the grated Pecorino Romano. Slice and serve.

Pistachio Pesto

1 cup unsalted, shelled pistachio nuts

½ cup olive oil, divided

8 cloves fresh garlic, peeled and coarsely chopped

1 cup heavy cream

2 ounces (57 grams) grated Pecorino Romano cheese (you can substitute Parmesan, but Pecorino Romano is preferred) (about 1 cup)

1 cup fresh basil leaves, tightly packed

2 tablespoons lemon juice

Salt and pepper

In a dry skillet, toast the pistachio nuts over medium heat, stirring to prevent burning, until the nuts are aromatic and too hot to touch. Alternatively, toast them on a sheet pan in a 375°F oven for 6 to 8 minutes. Transfer them into a bowl and set aside to cool.

Place ¼ cup of the olive oil into a hot skillet, heating the oil for a few seconds until it shimmers. Stir in the chopped garlic for 3 to 5 seconds, then immediately stir the garlic and oil into the bowl with the pistachios.

Place the remaining oil, as well as the cream, grated cheese, basil leaves, and lemon juice, into a food processor and add the garlic and nut mixture. Process for 20 to 30 seconds, until the ingredients form a coarse but evenly blended, spreadable sauce. Transfer to a bowl and add salt and pepper to taste. Refrigerate until 1 hour before use, then bring to room temperature so it's easier to spread.

Note: Pistachio Pesto can be prepared up to a day ahead and will keep for 4 to 5 days in the refrigerator.

Nicole Russell

"Kiss Mi' Converse" Jerk Chicken Pizza

Makes 2 (16-inch) or 3 (14-inch) pizzas

Last Dragon Pizza is the creation of Nicole Russell, who lives in Rockaway, Queens, and who reinvented herself after the devastation from Hurricane Sandy left her jobless. Her childhood love of pizza and the movie *The Last Dragon* inspired her to start making pizzas for the locals, who happily spread the word, and before long, she was being featured on television and was even invited to accompany a delegation of pizza luminaries, sponsored by Orlando Foods and the Caputo Flour company, on a tour of Italy. Suddenly, she became everyone's protégé, and her business, still based in her home, exploded. Customers have been happy to schedule their pickups around Nicole's limited ability to meet the demand out of her small oven. Here's what she told me about the pizza featured here:

> If I were to pick a signature pizza pie from Last Dragon Pizza that would best represent the brand and the overall concept, it would be the "Kiss Mi' Converse." As you know, Last Dragon Pizza is inspired by the '80's cult classic film, The Last Dragon. *All of our pies are named after memorable scenes and characters from the movie.*
>
> When coming up with the menu, I knew I had to have classic pizza choices like pepperoni and of course the Margherita that Raffaele Esposito created for Queen Margherita—a pizza emulating the red, white, and green of the Italian flag. So, being a pizza-making woman of Jamaican descent, I created the "Kiss Mi' Converse" jerk chicken pizza that gives consumers a taste of my heritage, using toppings that also represent the colors of the Jamaican flag: Black, green, and gold.
>
> The key ingredients to authentic Jamaican jerk sauce are: powdered pimento berries (or ground allspice berries), scallions, and yellow or orange Scotch bonnet peppers. Using a mortar and pestle, Jamaican women grind these ingredients, making the foundation of the sauce. They then grind in garlic, cinnamon, nutmeg, and thyme. Next comes salt, sugar, and black pepper to taste.
>
> The men in my family would handle the smoking of the meat; that is, as they say, "the jerking." A lot of folks think the key to jerk chicken is the sauce or marinade. But nope, the key to authentic Jamaican jerk is the long smoking process using pimento wood, twigs, leaves, etc. Everything about jerk is all about pimento. So if you want to take jerk chicken up a notch, source some really good pimento wood online.
>
> There's a memorable scene in The Last Dragon *where the villain, Sho'Nuff, tells the hero of the film, Bruce Leroy, to "Bow down and 'Kiss My Converse!'" A common phrase that's often used by Jamaicans when they can't believe something, or are shocked, is, "Kiss Mi' Neck Back!" Hence my play on the words. The pizza is comprised of a traditional plain cheese pizza base: dough, sauce, and mozzarella cheese. But the topping includes chicken marinated in my personal jerk sauce recipe, and*

tossed with sweet white onions, black olives, and yellow bell peppers. The pizza is topped with green scallion strips laid in an "x" formation in the center of the pie (or several x's) to complete the nod to the Jamaican flag.

Thank you, Nicole.

For this version I won't expect you to smoke your chicken over pimento wood, or even make your own jerk marinade (though I've provided a recipe should you choose to do so), but I think this tribute fulfills the spirit of Nicole's intent to honor Jamaica and all it means to her.

½ teaspoon salt

4 boneless chicken thighs or 2 boneless chicken breasts (note smoked chicken option below)

Jerk Marinade (recipe follows) or prepared jerk marinade

1 medium onion, julienned

New York Pizza Dough (page 30), made at least a day ahead

Crushed Tomato Pizza Sauce (page 42)

6 ounces (170 grams) whole milk mozzarella, shredded (about 1½ cups)

6 ounces (170 grams) low-fat mozzarella, shredded (about 1½ cups)

1 cup finely grated Pecorino Romano or Parmesan cheese

1 yellow bell pepper, medium diced

½ cup sliced black olives

2 scallions

Note: You can substitute 1 pound of smoked deli chicken (or smoked turkey) for the thigh or breast meat. Cut it into bite size pieces and marinate it as directed above.

The day before making the pizzas (or at least 3 hours before), fill a 3-quart pot ¾ full with water and add the salt. Bring the water to a gentle boil and add the chicken. Decrease the temperature to medium low and poach the chicken in the simmering water, gently stirring for 5 to 7 minutes, until firm to the touch. Remove the chicken with a slotted spoon and set in a bowl to cool while you make the marinade (recipe follows). Once the marinade is made, cut the chicken into bite-size pieces (about 1 inch) and return them to the bowl. Add the onion and pour the marinade over the chicken and onion. Stir to thoroughly coat all the pieces. Cover the bowl with plastic wrap and refrigerate.

Three hours before making the pizzas, remove the dough from the refrigerator and divide into 2 pieces for large pizzas or 3 pieces for medium pizzas, then roll them into tight dough balls. Lightly mist a sheet pan or dough box with vegetable oil spray and place the dough balls on the pan. Mist the top of the dough balls with the oil spray and loosely cover the pan with plastic wrap. Set the dough aside at room temperature to proof for about 3 hours. While the dough is proofing, make the tomato sauce and mix together the 2 types of mozzarella in one bowl.

An hour before making the pizzas, place a baking stone or baking steel on the middle oven rack and preheat to 550°F or as hot as the oven will allow. Make 1 pizza at a time, starting with stretching 1 dough ball (see page 18). Lightly dust a pizza peel with flour, semolina, or cornmeal, then transfer the dough to the peel.

Spread enough tomato sauce to lightly cover the surface (½ to ¾ cup, depending on the size of the dough), leaving an uncovered border of about ½ inch around the perimeter. Add a dusting of the Pecorino or Parmesan cheese, then distribute the shredded mozzarella over the surface, reserving enough for the other pizzas. Add the marinated chicken and onions, leaving the marinade on the pieces. Distribute the diced bell pepper pieces and sliced olives over the surface. Just before baking the pizzas, slice the scallions down the center into two thin strips, then cut them across into 4-inch lengths and set them aside.

Slide the pizza onto the baking stone or steel and bake for 4 minutes. Rotate 180 degrees and bake for an additional 4 to 6 minutes, until the cheese is bubbly and beginning to caramelize and the edge of the pizza (cornicione) is golden brown. The underside of the crust should also be golden brown. Remove the pizza and transfer it onto a cutting board. Form the cut scallions into 4 to 6 "x" formation on top of the pizza. Slice and serve.

Jerk Marinade

1 medium onion, quartered

4 scallions, cleaned and cut into big pieces

1 yellow bell pepper, quartered

1 Scotch bonnet or habanero pepper

4 garlic cloves, peeled

1 tablespoon brown sugar

1 tablespoon soy sauce

½ teaspoon kosher salt

½ teaspoon dried thyme, or 1 teaspoon fresh thyme

¼ teaspoon ground allspice or allspice berries

¼ teaspoon ground cinnamon

⅛ teaspoon ground nutmeg

⅛ teaspoon ground clove

⅛ teaspoon black pepper

Place all ingredients into a food processor and process continuously for 30 to 60 seconds, until the ingredients are fully broken down and form a thick paste.

The Concetta

Makes 4 (12-inch) pizzas

One of the enduring sound bites of my *Pizza Quest* interview with Anthony Mangieri is when he looked straight at the camera and said, "I don't compromise." I love that shot.

Ever since he launched his pizzeria, Una Pizza Napoletana, more than 25 years ago, Anthony has been known as a singular purist, whether it be the wood-fired ovens he builds himself, the naturally leavened dough, or the minimalist menu with no substitutions, all in an obsessive pursuit of excellence in every pie. Anthony is also an innately spiritual person who has a devotional connection to his pizzas. Here's what he told me about the Concetta Pizza, featured here:

I name all my special pizzas after an important woman in my life. This one is for my Aunt Concetta. She was always considered the family cook/baker. She just had that magic touch. She and I would talk often when I was younger, and she was a big influence on me. This pizza is all about the dough and really highlighting the amazing tomatoes from the Campania region of Italy, the area my family comes from. It's got four different varieties of tomatoes: San Marzano DOP, Corbarino, Piennolo, and sun-dried. Along with breadcrumbs, Pecorino cheese, and parsley. It also really plays on the staples of the Italian American kitchen.

My tribute version is designed to capture the essence of The Concetta, knowing full well that most home cooks won't be able to find all the imported tomato varieties and specialty ingredients Anthony has sourced. But this version will get you pretty darn close, especially if you can connect with your own local or favorite ingredients the way Anthony does. Often, it's the connection between the pizza maker and the ingredients they love that is conveyed to those eating it. As we've seen in all the pizzas in this book, it's the love as much as the tomatoes that they will experience and remember, which I think is the real secret behind the success of Anthony Mangieri.

Sourdough Pizza Dough (page 32, purist version), made at least a day ahead

28-ounce can San Marzano-style whole plum tomatoes

16 ounces (454 grams) fresh heirloom, grape, and/or cherry tomatoes

1 jar marinated sun-dried tomatoes

1 tablespoon olive oil

1½ teaspoons kosher, coarse, or flake sea salt (such as Maldon), divided

1 teaspoon dried oregano

1 teaspoon dried basil

½ teaspoon dried thyme

1 small bunch of Italian parsley, washed and coarsely chopped

1 teaspoon coarse or flake salt

2 cups dried, unseasoned bread crumbs, such as Panko

4 ounces (113 grams) grated Pecorino Romano cheese (2 cups)

Four hours before baking, remove the dough from the refrigerator and divide it into 4 (9-ounce/255-gram) pieces. Shape them into tight balls. Mist a sheet pan or dough box with vegetable or olive oil spray and place the dough balls on the pan or in the dough box. Mist the top of the dough balls with the spray and cover loosely with plastic wrap. Set aside at room temperature to proof for about 4 hours.

While the dough is proofing, puree the canned tomatoes in a food processor or blender, add salt and pepper to taste, and transfer to a bowl. Cover and refrigerate.

Slice the heirloom tomatoes into 1-inch cubes and halve or quarter the smaller tomatoes. Cut the sun-dried tomatoes into bite-size pieces, reserving the marinade. Combine all tomatoes in a bowl. Add the marinade from the sun-dried tomatoes along with the olive oil, ½ teaspoon of the salt, and dried oregano, basil, and thyme. Gently stir the tomatoes with the marinade to coat them. Cover with plastic wrap and refrigerate.

An hour before making the pizzas, place a baking stone or baking steel on the middle oven rack and preheat to 550°F or as hot as the oven will allow. When it's time to bake the pizzas, begin stretching the dough balls (see page 18) to about 12 inches in diameter. Assemble 1 pizza at a time, preparing the next while the previous one is baking.

Lightly dust a pizza peel with flour, semolina, or cornmeal, then transfer the dough to the peel. Cover the surface of the dough with about ½ cup of the pureed canned tomatoes, leaving a ½-inch rim around the perimeter uncovered. Evenly distribute one-quarter of the sliced fresh tomato mixture over the surface. Distribute ¼ cup of the chopped parsley over the tomatoes. Sprinkle ¼ teaspoon of salt over the surface.

Slide the pizza into the oven and bake for about 4 minutes. Use the peel to rotate 180 degrees and continue baking for 2 to 4 minutes, until the edge of the crust is puffy and golden brown, and the underside is also golden brown. Transfer the pizza onto a cutting board and top with a generous dusting of the bread crumbs (about ½ cup) and ½ cup of grated Pecorino Romano. Slice and serve.

Si's Special with Kettle Chips

Makes 3 (14-inch) pizzas

I first met Siler Chapman when I moved to Charlotte, North Carolina, in 2003 and heard about a local wunderkind who was tearing it up in international acrobatic dough-tossing competitions. Siler is yet another Tony Gemignani protégé, plucked from the crowd by Tony and invited to join his team because of Siler's natural athletic ability, easy coachability, and boundless energy—I can see why Tony took him on. Fast-forward 18 years, and Siler is now a family man, longtime pizzeria operator (both independent and onetime franchise owner), and consultant, and he's now part of the next-generation artisan pizza movement. Like his mentor, Tony, he has moved beyond dough-tossing competitions and is now perfecting his own pizza craft via his multi-unit mobile pizza business, King of Fire, and training his own crew of protégés, including my own nephew, Chris Reinhart (page 97). King of Fire pizzas have risen to the top of the local "best of" pyramid, and the menu features a number of fun and inventive options, such as this popular favorite, known as Si's Special, where the crunch of potato chips serves as a total game changer. Unlike many of the other tribute pizzas in this book, which depend on prepping homemade ingredients, this one is made from an aggregate of easily found commercial ingredients, yet provides a total wow factor and makes this Si's pizza, well, special.

Classic White Dough (page 26), made at least a day ahead

12 slices hickory-smoked bacon

9 ounces (255 grams) precooked breaded chicken nuggets, bites, or tenders, any brand (can be frozen)

6 ounces (170 grams) whole milk mozzarella, shredded (about 1½ cups)

6 ounces (170 grams) low-fat (part skim) mozzarella, shredded (about 1½ cups)

1 (8-ounce/227-gram) bag kettle-fried (thick cut) potato chips, any brand, broken into coarse crumbles

Ranch dressing (any brand, or use the recipe that follows for Susan's Ranch Dressing)

Hot sauce (Sweet Baby Ray's, Frank's, Texas Pete, or other brand)

Three hours before baking, remove the dough from the refrigerator and divide it into 3 (12-ounce/340-gram) pieces. Lightly mist a sheet pan or dough box with vegetable oil spray. Form the pieces into tight dough balls and place them on the pan or in the dough box. Mist the top of the dough balls with the spray and loosely cover with plastic wrap. Set aside to proof at room temperature for about 3 hours.

Preheat the oven to 400° F. Line 1 or 2 sheet pans with baking parchment, then place the bacon slices on the sheet pan(s) and bake on the middle rack for 10 to 15 minutes, until the bacon lightly browns and starts to crisp but is still flexible. While bacon is baking, line a platter with a paper towel. Transfer the baked slices to the platter and set it aside to cool, saving the bacon fat for future use. When the bacon has cooled, chop it into coarse pieces, about ¾ inch long. Defrost the breaded chicken pieces (if necessary) and set them aside or refrigerate them. Mix the whole milk and low-fat mozzarella in a bowl, then cover and refrigerate.

An hour before making the pizzas, place a baking stone or baking steel on the middle oven rack and preheat to 550°F. Stretch out one pizza dough to 14 inches in diameter (see page 18). Lightly dust a pizza peel with flour, semolina, or cornmeal, then transfer the dough to the peel. Distribute one-third of the shredded cheese (about 1 cup) over the surface of the dough, leaving a rim of ½ inch around the perimeter without cheese.

Cut the breaded chicken into 1 to 1½-inch nuggets and distribute ⅓ of the pieces over the surface of the pizza. Sprinkle the bacon pieces over the chicken, followed by about 1 cup of crumbled potato chips.

Slide the pizza onto the stone and bake for 4 minutes, then rotate 180 degrees and continue to bake for 2 to 4 additional minutes, until the cheese is bubbly and caramelized, and the crust is golden brown around the edge (cornicione) and golden on the underside. Transfer the pizza to a cutting board. Generously drizzle the ranch dressing over the chicken and bacon, then sprinkle on streaks or drops of the hot sauce. Cut and serve.

Susan's Ranch Dressing

My wife, Susan, makes a killer ranch dressing, so we rarely buy commercial brands. You might not be able to go back either once you try it.

½ cup mayonnaise

½ cup sour cream

½ cup buttermilk

1 tablespoon lemon juice

¼ teaspoon kosher or fine sea salt

¼ teaspoon black pepper

¼ teaspoon dried onion powder

¼ teaspoon granulated garlic

¼ teaspoon celery seeds (whole or ground)

2 teaspoons dried chives, or ¼ cup diced scallions or chives

Whisk together all ingredients, adding the chives or scallions last. Adjust salt and pepper to taste. Let it sit for at least 1 hour before using. Refrigerate any leftover dressing; it will keep for at least 1 week.

Chris Reinhart

The Low Country Pizza

Makes 3 (14-inch) pizzas

Full disclosure: This guy is my nephew, but he's paid his pizza dues over the past ten years. After graduating from Johnson & Wales University, Chris was part of the opening team at Pie Town and, later, on the opening team at Pure Pizza, two of Charlotte, North Carolina's landmark pizzerias, where I served as a menu and training consultant. He put in a few more development years working as a manager for Grant Arons at Inizio and then at Eight & Sand (see page 83), before joining Siler Chapman at King of Fire (see page 94), and, most recently, joined his best friend, Austin Crum, at Izzy's, where they crank out bar pizzas in a food truck in the beer garden of the Triple C Brewery tasting room. Chris and Austin also create pizzas for various beer and pizza pairing events, such as this one developed by Chris for a special event.

    The pie featured here is a favorite of mine because I'm a huge fan of what is called, "down in these here parts," the Low Country Boil. It's a spicy shrimp, sausage, potato, and corn extravaganza extremely popular in the coastal areas of the Carolinas (and exists under various names in other parts of the country). Chris took the logical step (for a pizzaiolo) of translating this concept into a spectacular pizza in which whatever beer is being featured during the dinner is also used as part of the shrimp boil (or you could just drink it while you're cooking). You won't find this pizza on the daily menu, but it might be available for private events if you give Izzy's a call.

Classic White Dough (page 26), made at least a day ahead

Low Country Boil (recipe follows)

12 ounces (340 grams) whole milk mozzarella cheese, shredded (about 6 cups)

1 red bell pepper, seeded and julienned

½ cup finely chopped Italian parsley

1 organic lemon, cut into 6 wedges

Three hours before making the pizzas, remove the dough from the refrigerator and divide it into 3 (12-ounce/340-gram) pieces. Lightly mist a sheet pan or dough box with vegetable oil spray. Form the dough pieces into tight dough balls and place them on the pan or in the dough box. Mist the dough balls with spray and cover loosely with plastic wrap. Set aside at room temperature to proof for about 3 hours.

An hour before making the pizzas, place a baking stone or baking steel on the middle oven rack and preheat to 550°F or as hot as the oven will allow. While the oven is preheating, remove the pan of Low Country Boil ingredients and separate them, placing each into its own bowl or on plates. Cut or shave the kernels from the corncobs (or collect the niblets). If cutting, try to keep the kernels together in sheets or patches. Peel the shrimp and cut them in half lengthwise; if any of the seasoning sticks to the ingredients, leave it on.

When it's time to make the pizzas, lightly dust a pizza peel with flour, semolina, or cornmeal and stretch out your first dough ball (see page 18) to 14 inches in diameter. Distribute 4 ounces (113 grams/about 1 cup) of mozzarella over the surface of the pizza, followed by ⅓ of the corn kernels or corn clusters. Add ⅓ each of the potato quarters and the uncooked slivers of bell pepper. Finally, distribute ⅓ of the andouille slices and shrimp.

Slide the pizza onto the baking stone and bake for 4 minutes, then rotate 180 degrees and continue baking for 2 to 4 additional minutes, until the cheese is melted and bubbly and the crust is golden brown on the edge (cornicione) and on the underside.

Transfer the pizza to a cutting board and garnish with the parsley. Slice and serve with two lemon wedges, or squeeze the wedges over the pizza before serving.

Low Country Boil

12-ounce bottle of beer

½ cup Old Bay Seasoning

6 small to medium red potatoes, washed and quartered

3 ears fresh, shucked corn on the cob*, or 1½ cups frozen niblets

2 links andouille sausage, sliced into ¼-inch discs

12 large shrimp, shell on, deveined

*Chris prefers to shave off sections (or patches) of corn, as pictured

To prepare the Low Country Boil, bring 3 quarts of water to a boil in a large pot and add the beer and the seasoning. Decrease heat to medium-high and maintain a gentle boil. Add the potatoes and simmer for 5 minutes. Add the corn on the cob (if using niblets, add those later, at the end) and continue simmering for another 5 minutes. Add the andouille and continue simmering for another 5 minutes. Bring the pot back to a rolling boil during the final minute and add the shrimp (and the niblets if using). Immediately remove the pot from the heat and wait 5 minutes, then drain the contents into a large colander. Spread the ingredients onto a sheet pan and cool at room temperature for 15 minutes, then place the pan in the refrigerator to continue cooling.

Adam Kuban

Classic Bar Pizza

Makes 6 (9-inch) or 4 (12-inch) pizzas

Adam Kuban is one of the breakout stars of food blogging. His posts on *Slice* (which he founded in 2003), *A Hamburger Today* (which he co-founded), and *Serious Eats* (which bought his two other sites and made him its founding food editor) years ago established his street cred as a serious national voice. When I finally met him in person, over a crispy Detroit–style pie at Brooklyn's Emmy Squared, he filled me in on his latest obsession for old-time American "bar pizza" and told me about his occasional Monday night Margot's Pizza pop-ups at various pizzerias in Brooklyn, where he has built a following as he works on mastering this previously underestimated pizza classic. As a major influencer, Adam had a hand in the recent revival of this thin, crispy style, made in bars in regular restaurant ovens and full of cheesy goodness. He demonstrated his technique in a special *Pizza Talk* episode in which he, Brian Spangler, and John Arena all showcased their different approaches to this style, where I learned how the bar pizza, the tavern pizza, and the parlor pizza (think of Shakey's Pizza Parlor) are all variations on this theme, and guess what? By the time this book comes out, thanks to the passion of Adam and his followers, the bar pizza will be well into its second act, especially at microbreweries and on food trucks, where it's a perfect fit.

This tribute version incorporates as many of Adam's techniques as I could squeeze in and will allow you to make an excellent bar pizza, replete with bubbly, crackly crust, to turn your game days into popular gatherings (I'm assuming that by the time this book comes out such gatherings will be allowed again). After that, track him down at Margot's Pizza wherever it pops up, or head over to your nearest bar pizza hangout.

Notes

- Just to add fuel to the flames, Adam also contributed his pineapple and pepperoni variation, so let the heated "pineapple" discussions begin . . .

- You will need round pan pizza pans for this method, and they are easily obtained, with diameters of 9 inches, 10 inches, or 12 inches and a sidewall of 1½ inches. You can order nonstick LloydPans versions of these (highly advised) at various online retailers.

New York Pizza Dough for Slice and Bar Pizzas, using the Bar Pizza variation (page 30)

4 teaspoons solid vegetable shortening, unsalted butter, or lard

Crushed Tomato Pizza Sauce (page 42)

1 tablespoon dried minced onions

3 ounces (85 grams) Romano cheese, grated (about ¾ cup)

8 ounces (227 grams) white cheddar cheese, shredded

8 ounces (227 grams) whole milk mozzarella, shredded (about 4 cups)

4 ounces (113 grams) fontina cheese, shredded (about 2 cups)

3 teaspoons dried oregano

2 tablespoons olive oil

18 fresh basil leaves

2 ounces (57 grams) Parmesan cheese, grated (about ½ cup)

Pineapple and Pepperoni Variation

24-ounce can crushed or sliced pineapple, drained

6 ounces (170 grams) cupping pepperoni or other cured salami, such as soppressata or Calabrese salami, sliced thin

Four hours before baking, remove the dough from the refrigerator and divide it into 6 (6-ounce/170-gram) pieces for 9-inch or 10-inch pans, or 4 (9-ounce/255-gram) pieces for a 12-inch pan. Lightly mist a sheet pan or dough box with vegetable oil spray. Form the dough pieces into tight dough balls and place them on the pan or in the dough box. Mist the tops with the spray, cover loosely with plastic wrap or a lid, and set aside at room temperature to proof for about 2½ hours.

While the dough is proofing, combine the tomato sauce and dried minced onions. Drain the pineapple and slice the pepperoni or salami, if using.

Use ½ teaspoon of shortening, butter, or lard to grease a ½-inch band around the outer perimeter of the pans' surfaces. Rub another ½ teaspoon over the entire inside surface of the pans, including the interior walls, or mist all of the inner surfaces with pan spray, but don't omit the ½-band using the solid fat. Set the pans aside.

After 2½ hours of proofing, lightly dust a work surface with all-purpose flour to begin rolling out the dough balls. Dust each dough ball with the flour, and flatten each with your hand. Working from the center outward, use a rolling pin to work each dough ball into a flat circle (see page 20), rotating the dough as you roll it and lifting it from time to time to break the contact with the work surface. Dust with more flour as needed. Roll out each piece as far as it will allow without springing back, then move on to the next piece. The pieces will, at first, only extend to about 6 inches in diameter, but they'll extend further after they rest.

After you finish rolling them all, return to the first dough and roll it out again, from the center to the perimeter, repeating the process with all the doughs until they are all the full diameter of the pans. You can stack the dough circles in a pile, with a light dusting of flour in between each, if you need room to work. When they're all rolled out, transfer them one at a time into the prepared pans, pressing the outer edge of the dough into the pan so the band of fat anchors the dough in place, preventing it from shrinking away from the walls of the pan. (If you don't have enough pans, stack the rolled-out extra doughs on a floured plate, cover with plastic wrap, and refrigerate. They will keep for 24 hours; otherwise, freeze them.)

An hour before making the pizzas, place a baking stone or baking steel on the middle oven rack and preheat to 550°F or as hot as the oven will allow.

Use a fork or a docking tool to prick holes across the surface of the dough to prevent large bubbles or pocketing. Spread enough tomato sauce over the surface to cover it generously, but not excessively (¼ to ½ cup per pizza, depending on the diameter). Sprinkle ¼ to ½ teaspoon of oregano over the sauce. Then sprinkle Romano cheese over the sauce—about ½ ounce (14 grams or 1 tablespoon) for 9-inch pizzas; 1 ounce (28 grams or 2 tablespoons) for 12-inch pizzas.

Evenly divide the cheddar cheese into 2 bowls. Combine all the mozzarella and fontina in another bowl, tossing to evenly distribute. Cover the outer perimeter of each pizza with a ½-inch ring of shredded cheddar cheese to form a border, then distribute the mozzarella/fontina cheese blend over the surface of each pizza. Drizzle 1 teaspoon of olive oil over each pizza (or, if making the pineapple pepperoni variation, distribute those ingredients over the top instead of the olive oil).

Depending on the size of the oven and the pans, place one or more of the pizzas in the oven, directly on the baking stone, and bake for 6 to 8 minutes, rotating 180 degrees after the first 4 minutes for a more even bake. When the cheese around the border turns golden brown and the overall cheese begins to bubble and slightly brown, remove the pans from the oven and place them on a heat-resistant surface, such as the stovetop.

Run a metal spatula around the perimeter of the pizzas to release them from the pans. Using the spatula, slide each pizza from the pan back onto the pizza peel (the pizzas will still be limp and floppy at this point). Return each pizza to the oven, directly onto the baking stone. Bake for about 1 minute, or until the underside of the crust turns golden brown and begins to crisp. Transfer the pizzas to a cutting board. Roll up 3 leaves of basil per pizza and use kitchen shears to cut slivers of basil over the surface of each pizza. Top with grated Parmesan to taste. Slice the pizza into wedges (bar style) or cut into squares (tavern style or "party cut") and serve.

Square and Other Pan Pizzas

Audrey Sherman Kelly

The Patty-Style Grandma Pizza

Makes 1 (12 by 18-inch) pan pizza

Audrey Jane Sherman Kelly is the founder of Audrey Jane's Pizza Garage in Boulder, Colorado, and a rising superstar in the pizza community because of her fabulous pizzas, her articles in *Pizza Today* magazine, and her competition victories. She makes round slice pies as well as Sicilian and Grandma square pizzas at the Garage. When she appeared on *Pizza Talk*, she talked about the emotional connection she has with her Grandma pizza, The Patty–Style. I'll let her explain:

> The Patty–style pizza that we make is an ode to my mom. It is named after her and based on the pizza she used to make for my siblings and me when we were growing up. It is, what I now realize, a version of a Grandma–style pizza, meaning aged dough pressed into a pan, drenched with extra virgin olive oil and laced with a sesame seed bottom. The dough becomes pillowy soft from rising in the pan, and the sesame seeds combine with the olive oil to provide an ample crunch. It definitely has that signature buttery-fried taste of a Grandma pie with a little something extra.
>
> My mom grew up in an Italian American family in Colorado, and her father, allegedly, had ties to the Pueblo mob. When she would make this pie, it was not from a specific recipe and certainly not called Grandma–style. It was from an innate memory she held, passed down to my mom from her grandmother, and from her to me.
>
> I have tried making this pizza many ways and one of the beautiful things about it is that it's hard to screw up. You can push it out in the pan and let it rise for a few hours or even overnight. You can par-bake it and then add the toppings for the second bake. If you are pressed for time or need a last-minute dinner idea, it is just as good stretched, topped raw, and baked without a decent rise. As long as you have properly fermented dough, it will pop in the oven without an extended proof. While it is definitely one of our best sellers at the restaurant, it also is a fantastic pizza to make at home. My favorite version is simply topped with whole milk mozzarella, crushed tomato sauce, basil, parmesan, and extra virgin olive oil. The secret to having it come out perfect is to use the best versions of these ingredients.

One of the signature aspects of Audrey's version of this New York classic is the sesame seed under-crust. It makes so much sense ("Intuitively obvious to even the most casual observer," as a friend of mine put it), that I expect to see it in use everywhere right about . . . now.

Pan Pizza Dough (page 28), made at least a day ahead

3 tablespoons olive oil, divided

½ cup sesame seeds

6 ounces (170 grams) whole milk mozzarella cheese, sliced ⅛-inch thick at the deli

6 ounces (170 grams) Crushed Tomato Pizza Sauce (page 42)

16 large fresh basil leaves

6 cloves fresh garlic, sliced thin and covered with a drizzle of olive oil

3 ounces (85 grams) Parmesan or Romano cheese, grated (about 1 cup)

Optional toppings (see notes)

Five hours before baking pizza, remove the dough from the refrigerator. Line a 12 by 18-inch sheet pan with baking parchment or a silicone baking pan liner. Rub 1½ tablspoons of the olive oil over the baking surface and the inner sidewalls of the pan. Evenly distribute the sesame seeds over the surface of the pan. Transfer the whole dough into the center of the pan and rub olive oil over the exposed area to prevent sticking as you press out the dough with your fingertips and "dimple" it. The dough will cover only about ⅔ of the surface, then will start to spring back. Loosely cover the pan with plastic wrap or an inverted sheet pan and let it rest at room temperature for 20 minutes.

Uncover the pan, brush a small amount of olive oil on the surface of the dough and dimple the dough again from the center to the outer corners and sides, until it starts to spring back. Cover and rest the dough for another 20 minutes, then repeat the dimpling. Rest it yet again for 20 minutes and dimple it again (usually the dough will cover the surface after 3 dimpling cycles, but sometimes it takes 4). Once the dough has evenly covered the surface of the pan, cover the pan with plastic wrap and set it aside to proof at room temperature for 3 to 4 hours or until you plan to bake the pizza. (You can also refrigerate the rising pan of dough after 2 hours, removing it from the refrigerator 2 hours before baking the pizza to complete its rise.)

Preheat the oven to 475°F, or 425°F if using a convection oven. Brush the top of the dough with olive oil and dimple the dough one more time to make it even across the surface. Cover the surface of the dough with the mozzarella, leaving uncovered a ½-inch border around the perimeter. Spread the tomato sauce over the surface of the cheese, but not on the uncovered rim. Place 8 of the basil leaves evenly over the sauce, then distribute the oiled garlic slices or other optional toppings over the basil leaves.

Place the pan on the bottom oven rack (see note) and bake for about 11 minutes. Rotate 180 degrees and continue baking for 10 to 12 minutes, until the cheese is bubbling through the sauce and the edge of the pizza is a rich golden brown. Bake longer if needed, but remove pizza from the oven if the cheese or the crust turn dark brown.

Remove the pizza from the oven and place it on the stovetop or other heat-resistant surface (not wood or vinyl). Place the remaining 8 basil leaves over the surface of the pizza. Sprinkle the Parmesan or Romano cheese over the top, then drizzle the remaining olive oil over the whole pizza. Use a metal bench or pastry blade, or a metal offset spatula, to trace around the outer perimeter of the crust, separating it from the pan. Use the pastry blade or a large metal spatula to get under the crust and gently guide the pizza onto a large cutting board. (If the parchment or silicon pad sticks to the pizza, don't worry; you can separate it from the crust after the transfer,) Slice into squares and serve.

Notes: Various toppings (pepperoni, onions, sausage, vegetables, chopped garlic, mushrooms, etc.) can be added to the top of the pizza, to taste, before baking.

For this pizza, the lower rack in the oven is preferred because it will provide more direct heat to the underside of the crust. However, if the pizza seems to be baking too quickly on the underside, you can move the pan up to the middle rack.

Chris Decker

The Sicilian

Makes 1 (12 by 18-inch) pizza

Chris Decker is John Arena's longtime right-hand man at Metro Pizza in Las Vegas, but he is emerging as a force in his own right, no longer the Robin to John's Batman. He has recently been interviewed and written about a number of times in pizza magazines, has been listed as one of the 50 most influential pizza makers in America, has been winning his fair share of pizza competitions, and is becoming known in the trade as the new generation Sicilian pizza king. Chris has been absorbing pizza wisdom for over thirty years while working with John and is connecting all the dots to forge his unique application of dough science and practiced technique to create signature pies within the larger Metro umbrella (Metro Pizza, by the way, is so named because it pays tribute to a number of metropolitan styles, from New York to Naples, Detroit to California cuisine). Chris, while adept at all these styles, has really honed in on the Sicilian pan-style, aiming for a light and airy crust, with lots of crunch and custard-like creaminess in the interior. It's not as easy as he makes it look, but this tribute version will get you started.

Here's what Chris says about his method:

It is made with a five-day cold ferment, 14-hour proof, and is a Sicilian pizza that looks like a brick, but feels like a feather. Easily digested and with a great contrast in mouth-feel, with the bottom being super crunchy, as it's almost "fried" in the pan with Corto (American) olive oil, and soft as a pillow in the middle. I feel that the perfect topping is Rosa Grande cup and char pepperoni and some fresh basil.

The following version will work with a simple overnight fermentation, but I recommend giving the dough 4 or even 5 days of cold fermentation before panning it, as Chris does. The added fermentation time helps tenderize the gluten and develop a more complex flavor but does slow down the final rising time.

Pan Pizza Dough (page 28), preferably made at least 4 days ahead

4 ounces (113 grams) olive oil, divided

3 ounces (85 grams) full-fat mozzarella cheese, shredded

3 ounces (85 grams) fontina or provolone cheese, shredded

1 cup Crushed Tomato Pizza Sauce (page 42)

18 large fresh basil leaves

4 ounces (113 grams) or 1 cup sliced cupping pepperoni

Six hours before baking the pizzas, remove the dough from the refrigerator. Line a 12 by 18-inch sheet pan with baking parchment or a silicon baking pad. and use 1½ tablespoons of olive oil to generously oil the surface of the pan and the inside walls. Transfer the dough to the oiled pan, rub the top with olive oil, and begin dimpling it. It will probably cover only a third to half of the pan. Rub the surface with more olive oil and cover the pan loosely with plastic wrap. Let the dough rest at room temperature for 20 minutes, then dimple it again and set it aside to rest. It will take 3 or 4 dimpling cycles at 20-minute intervals for the dough to fully cover the surface of the pan. Once the pan is evenly filled by the dough, rub or brush olive oil over the surface, cover it with plastic wrap, and let it proof at room temperature for about 4 hours. The dough will bubble and rise and be very soft and fragile, so handle it gently when you move the pan.

Preheat the oven to 475°F. Place the pan of dough on the middle rack and bake for 10 minutes. Rotate 180 degrees and continue baking for 6 to 8 minutes, until the dough is springy to the touch, golden brown on top, and caramelized to a light to medium golden brown on the underside. Remove the pan from the oven and set it aside to cool. You can make the final pizza immediately, on the still-hot crust, or you can store the crust for up to 5 days in the refrigerator, wrapped, or up to 3 months in the freezer.

While the crust is baking, mix the cheeses together in a bowl and set it aside or refrigerate it.

When you're ready to bake, preheat the oven to 500°F. Spread the tomato sauce over the baked crust, leaving a ½-inch border around the perimeter uncovered. Evenly distribute the cheese mixture over the sauce, again leaving a ½-inch border uncovered. Roll up 12 of the basil leaves and cut them into slivers with a knife (chiffonade) or with kitchen shears, then sprinkle them over the cheese. Distribute the pepperoni over the surface of the pizza. Place the pan on the middle rack of the oven and bake for 5 minutes. Rotate 180 degrees and continue baking for 3 to 5 minutes, until the cheese is bubbling and caramelizing into a golden brown. Remove the pizza from the oven and place the pan on a heat-resistant surface, such as the stovetop.

Use a metal bench or pastry blade to trace around the perimeter of the pizza, separating it from the pan. Use the bench blade or a metal spatula to lift and guide the pizza from the pan onto a cutting board. If the parchment or silicone pad is still stuck to the underside, carefully lift the corner of the pizza and begin peeling it off after it's transferred to the cutting board. Garnish by cutting the remaining basil leaves into slivers, as before, and sprinkling them over the top. Let the pizza cool for 3 to 4 minutes, then cut it into squares and serve.

Justin DeLeon

The Acapulco Gold Crown Pizza

Makes 2 (10 by 14-inch) or 4 (8 by 8-inch) pan pizzas

The Acapulco Gold Crown Pizza, created by Justin DeLeon at his Apollonia's Pizzeria in Los Angeles, has become an Instagram sensation. Justin had been a successful photographer prior to going all-in on pizza, so this dramatic looking—and delicious—pizza is the perfect convergence of his skills.

I first heard about him during a *Pizza Talk* interview with Nancy Silverton, owner of Pizzeria Mozza (one of my top five pizzerias in the world), who told me she met Justin at a street festival in downtown L.A. in which they were both showcasing their work. Justin's daughter, Apollonia, with the innocent courage of a proud child, approached and asked her to come "taste my daddy's pizza." Nancy did and was duly impressed and suggested I include Justin in our interviews and, thus, in this collection.

In Justin's version of Detroit–style pizza, a generous border of cheddar cheese around the perimeter of the pan bakes up into a lacy, crispy *frico* as it climbs the walls of the pan. One trick that helps with the crown is to dry the cheese a bit by spreading it on a sheet pan, uncovered, in the refrigerator for a day or two before making the pizza, so it performs like a Parmesan cheese crisp or Florentine lace cookie. Whatever the analogy, this makes a conversation-stopping presentation, as you will see in this tribute version.

Sourdough Pizza Dough, made at least a day ahead, using the "pan pizza" adjustment and the instant yeast option (page 32)

Butter paste (page 11)

8 ounces (227 grams) mild cheddar cheese, shredded (about 4 cups), and dried overnight in the refrigerator

8 ounces (227 grams) brick cheese or whole milk mozzarella, shredded (about 4 cups)

2 cups golden (such as Acapulco Gold) or red cherry and/or grape tomatoes, halved

2 teaspoons flake salt, such as Maldon (or coarse salt)

2 cups ricotta cheese, whipped until smooth

2 ounces (57 grams) Parmesan or Romano cheese, grated

4 teaspoons truffle oil

Five hours before baking the crusts, remove the dough from the refrigerator and divide it into 2 (18-ounce/510-gram) pieces, or 4 (9-ounce/255-gram) pieces. Brush the inside of 2 pans, including the inside walls, with the butter paste. If not using all the dough, return the unused dough to the refrigerator in an oiled, covered bowl; it can keep for up to 4 days.

Place 1 piece of dough in a pan and, with oiled fingers, dimple it. Repeat the dimpling cycle 2 or 3 times at 20-minute intervals, until the dough fills the pan. Cover the pan with plastic wrap and set aside to proof for 4 hours at room temperature. The dough will double in size and be bubbly.

Preheat the oven to 500°F. Bake the pan of dough on the middle rack for 6 minutes. Rotate and continue baking for an additional 6 to 9 minutes, until the dough is golden brown on both the top and the underside. Transfer the dough from the pan onto a cutting board and let the pan cool, but do not wipe it clean (you will use it again for the re-bake). The baked crusts can be used immediately or can be cooled, wrapped, and stored in the refrigerator for up to 4 days or in the freezer for up to 3 months.

When you're ready to bake the final pizzas, preheat the oven to 500°F. Brush the inside surfaces of the pans, including the sidewalls, with another layer of butter paste. Depending on the size of the pans, place ¼ to ½ cup cheddar in each pan and tilt and jiggle the pan to coat the side walls with a layer of the cheese. Place the baked crust back into the pan and spread a generous layer of cheddar (¾ cup to 1 cup) around the perimeter to make a collar of cheese about ½ inch high above the dough.

Mix the remaining cheddar into the mozzarella (if you're using brick cheese, you can omit the cheddar at this stage), then spread a layer of cheese over the surface of the pizza, using half the cheese for each pie (half as much if using the smaller pans). Distribute the tomatoes over each pizza, followed by a sprinkle of flake salt over the tomatoes.

Bake on the center oven rack for 6 minutes, then rotate 180 degrees and continue baking for an additional 6 to 9 minutes, until the cheese begins to caramelize and the cheese around the perimeter becomes a rich golden brown and forms a lacy crown shape around the edge.

Transfer the pan to a heat-resistant surface, such as the stovetop or a cooling rack, and let it sit for about 2 minutes for the cheese to set, then use a bench blade or large metal spatula to trace around the perimeter. Lift from under the pizza to transfer it from the pan onto a cutting board. Spoon or pipe 6 dollops of the whipped ricotta cheese, evenly spaced, over the pizza. Sprinkle the Parmesan or Romano over the surface, followed by a drizzle of 1 to 2 teaspoons of truffle oil over each pizza. Cut into 6 to 8 squares and serve.

Derrick Tung

USA Pizza Cup Winner Square Pie with Bacon Jam

Makes 4 (8 by 10-inch) pizzas

Throughout this book, I highlight pizza tree lineages that have emerged from a few "mother house" pizzerias or mentors. Certainly, Paulie Gee, in just a few years (twelve, as of this writing), has spawned a number of talented protégés, such as Mike Kurtz and Mark Bello, and Derrick Tung, who owns Paulie Gee's Logan Square in Chicago, is yet another. As Derrick told us during his *Pizza Talk* interview, Paulie gives him a lot of latitude to introduce his own concepts to the menu of his Chicago franchise.

Like so many new-generation pizza makers, after first excelling at classic Neapolitan styles, Derrick became enamored with the growing square pie revolution. After figuring out his method, he decided to enter one of his own creations at the United States Pizza Championships, and, as you already know from the title, he won the gold medal.

What made this pie break from the pack against all the other square pies in the competition? A number of factors, including his awesome crust and the inventiveness of the flavors on top, where you can see the eclectic influence of all that has come before in the Paulie Gee's world (yes, I'm talking about the now-ubiquitous Mike's Hot Honey and the always-popular pepperoni) along with Derrick's own addition to the pizza lexicon: bacon jam! Add lots of cheese, including ricotta, and you are looking at a championship pizza. When I asked Derrick what he calls it on the menu in case any readers swing by, he told me, "The US Pizza Cup Winner, what else?"

Note: Throughout this book, I have purposely not asked for anyone's personal recipes for signature toppings they created, in order to protect their proprietary secrets. Instead, I've offered my own versions, based on and inspired by their originals. After all, I'm just the cover band—Derrick is the Dominos, and this jam is his Layla. But this house band version will get you pretty darn close.

Pan Pizza Dough (page 28), made a least a day in advance

Butter paste (page 11)

Bacon Jam (recipe follows)

Crushed Tomato Pizza Sauce (page 42)

6 ounces (170 grams) mild or medium cheddar cheese, shredded (about 1½ cups)

10 ounces (284 grams) whole milk mozzarella, shredded (about 2½ cups)

6 ounces (170 grams) sliced cupping pepperoni (about 2 cups)

2 cups ricotta cheese, whipped until smooth and fluffy

½ cup grated Parmesan or Romano cheese

¼ cup Mike's Hot Honey (or substitute, page 67)

20 fresh basil leaves

Five hours before pre-baking the crusts, remove the dough from the refrigerator and divide it into 4 (9-ounce/255-gram) pieces. Brush the inside of the pans, including the inside walls, with the butter paste. (If not using all the dough, return the unused dough to the refrigerator in a lightly oiled, covered bowl; it can be kept for up to 4 days). Place 1 piece of the dough in each prepared pan and, with oiled fingers, dimple it. Repeat the dimpling cycles 2 or 3 times, at 20-minute intervals, until the dough evenly fills the pan. Cover the pan with plastic wrap and proof for 4 hours at room temperature. The dough will double or triple in size and become bubbly, but very fragile.

While the dough is rising, prepare the topping ingredients. An hour before baking the pizzas, preheat the oven to 500°F and bake the pan(s) of proofed dough on the middle rack for 7 minutes. Rotate 180 degrees and continue baking for an additional 7 to 9 minutes, until the dough is light brown on both the top and the underside. Transfer the dough with a metal spatula from the pan onto a cutting board and let the pan cool, but do not wipe it clean (you will use it again for the re-bake).

When it's time to bake the final pizzas, preheat the oven to 500°F. Brush the pans with more butter paste and return the prebaked crusts to the pans; there should be a slight gap between the crust and the pan due to shrinkage during the first bake. Distribute one-quarter of the cheddar around the perimeter, allowing some to fall in the gap around the dough to make a nice collar of cheese around the crust, sitting about ½ inch higher than the crust. Cover the remaining surface of the crust with about ⅔ cup of the mozzarella. Evenly distribute 12 slices of pepperoni over the surface, followed by 12 small dollops of the bacon jam. Place the pan on the middle rack and bake for 5 minutes, then rotate 180 degrees and continue baking for an additional 5 to 7 minutes, until the cheese is golden and bubbly in the center and crisp and caramelized around the perimeter.

Transfer the pan to a heat-resistant surface, such as the stovetop, and let the pizza cool for 3 minutes. Use a bench blade or metal spatula to trace around the perimeter of the pizza to release it from the pan, then transfer it to a cutting board. Pipe or spoon 6 dollops of the ricotta on the pizza, followed by a sprinkling of Parmesan or Romano. Drizzle the hot honey in streaks over the whole pizza. Roll up 5 basil leaves per pizza and chiffonade them (or cut with scissors) for garnish. Slice into 6 squares and serve.

Bacon Jam

16 ounces (454 grams) sliced
   bacon

2 medium yellow or white onions,
   diced

¼ cup brown sugar

2 tablespoons balsamic vinegar

Lay out the strips of bacon on 1 or 2 sheet pans and bake at 375°F for about 20 minutes, or until the strips turn golden brown and are crisp. Drain off the bacon fat into a large sauté or frying pan over medium heat. Add the diced onions to the bacon fat and stir periodically for 20 to 30 minutes, until the onions wilt and become translucent. Add the brown sugar and stir until it dissolves, then add the balsamic vinegar. The mixture will be very juicy. Decrease the heat to medium-low and continue to cook slowly, stirring every few minutes, for 25 to 30 minutes, to reduce the liquid to the consistency of honey or maple syrup, making a jam-like texture. Turn off the heat. Dice the crisped bacon, then stir the bacon bits into the onion mixture and set aside to cool at room temperature before refrigerating. (Note: This can be made 1 or 2 days in advance or while the dough in the pans is proofing.)

Jeff Smokevitch

Parma Italia Square Pie

Makes 2 (10 by 14-inch) pizzas

Brown Dog Pizza in Telluride, Colorado, has had a huge impact on me even though I've never been there. It was Jeff Smokevitch, a former ski bum transplanted from (where else?) Detroit, who set the pizza world ablaze from high up in the Rockies with his Detroit–style pizza served at Brown Dog and now, also, at Blue Pan Pizza in Denver. I was commissioned to emulate his pizza for a restaurant consulting project, and, sight unseen, I jumped down the Detroit–style rabbit hole and immersed myself in this style. I fell in love with it, developed some original methods of my own, and finally got to taste Jeff's pizza at Pizza Expo in Las Vegas in 2018. I was struck by how well the parbake/re-bake method—which he developed because of the lines of people waiting to buy his pizzas—actually worked. Until then, I didn't think it possible that the crust could retain the creamy, custard-like texture so critical to this style of pizza if baked twice. Jeff proved me wrong and showed us all, both in his demo classes at the Expo and during an interview on *Pizza Talk* where he and Shawn Randazzo did a tandem session, serving as commentators for each other's demos. It was kind of like a *Super Session*. (If any of you are old enough to remember the amazing studio album in the late 1960s by Stephen Stills, Al Kooper, and Mike Bloomfield, you will know what I mean—if not, bring it up on Pandora or Spotify. You can thank me later.)

While Shawn showcased his traditional single-bake method, Jeff focused on his re-bake method and, to be honest, it was impossible to say one was better than the other. Until Shawn's tragic passing (see page 123), I thought of them as the Coke and Pepsi, the Abbott and Costello, the Penn and Teller, the Simon and Garfunkel, or even the Lewis and Clark of the Detroit–style pizza world. And you can see their legacy in how many have followed their trailblazing path.

This Parma Italia was a first-place winner at an international pizza competition in Parma, Italy, in 2013, and with good reason. It delivers layer upon decadent layer of flavor, making it one of the signature pies on the Brown Dog menu, and you're about to find out why. Even this, my tribute band version of Jeff's original, will cause you to levitate with Rocky Mountain joy, as high in the sky as Telluride.

Pan Pizza Dough (page 28), made at least a day ahead

Butter paste (page 11)

1 cup Crushed Tomato Pizza Sauce (page 42)

2 ounces (57 grams) Parmesan cheese

6 ounces (170 grams) mild or medium sharp cheddar cheese, shredded (about 1½ cups)

12 ounces (340 grams) whole milk mozzarella (about 3 cups)

6 ounces (170 grams) smoked scamorza cheese, or smoked provolone, mozzarella, or cheddar, shredded (about 1½ cups)

4 ounces (113 grams) soppressata or other spicy salumi, such as capicola, sliced into 1½ by ½-inch strips

8 ounces (227 grams) burrata cheese

4 ounces (113 grams) thinly sliced prosciutto ham, cut into 1 to 1½-inch strips

1 cup coarsely chopped baby arugula

3 tablespoons olive oil

Six hours before baking the final pizzas, remove the dough from the refrigerator and divide it into 2 (19-ounce/239-gram) pieces. Brush the inside of 2 pans, including the inside walls, with the butter paste. (If not using all the dough, return the unused dough to the refrigerator in a lightly oiled, covered bowl; it can be used for up to 4 additional days or frozen for 3 months). Place the dough pieces in the prepared pans and, with oiled fingers, dimple it. Repeat the dimpling 3 more times, at 20-minute intervals, until the dough fills the pans. Once the pans are evenly filled, cover them with plastic wrap and let them proof for 4 hours at room temperature. The dough will double in size and become soft and bubbly.

While the dough is rising, prepare the toppings, and shave the Parmesan into thin, paper-like curls with a potato or cheese peeler, or on the long horizontal slits of a box grater.

Preheat the oven to 500°F. Place the pans of dough on the middle rack and bake for 8 minutes, then rotate 180 degrees and continue baking for 6 to 8 additional minutes, until the dough is fully baked and springy to the touch, a light golden brown on top and a light to medium golden brown on the underside. Remove the pans from the oven and use a metal spatula to transfer the baked crust from the pans and onto a cooling rack or cutting board for at least 15 minutes (or wrap and refrigerate for up to 4 days, or freeze for up to 3 months).

When it's time to bake the pizzas, preheat the oven to 500°F. Lightly re-grease the pans with the butter paste, then return the cooled crusts to the pans. Distribute a line of cheddar cheese around the perimeter of the crust so that some of it falls between the crust and the pan and forms a ½-inch collar around and above the crust. Then spread about ½ cup of the crushed tomato sauce over the surface (but not over the collar of cheese)—just enough to coat the crust, but not enough to form a puddle. ("Kiss the dough with the sauce," as they say.) Distribute 1 cup of the mozzarella over the sauce, followed by ½ cup of the scamorza. Scatter ½ cup of the soppressata strips over the surface.

Place the pan back in the oven for 8 minutes, rotate 180 degrees and continue baking for 5 to 7 minutes, until the cheese is fully melted and starting to caramelize to a rich golden brown. Remove the pan and place on a heat-resistant surface, such as the stovetop. Use a bench blade or metal spatula to transfer the pizza onto a cutting board. It should come out easily, since it was prebaked.

Pinch off pieces of burrata and drop them over the hot pizza, followed by strips of the prosciutto, then the shaved Parmesan curls. Sprinkle ½ cup of arugula over the top, then drizzle 1½ tablespoons of olive oil over the whole pizza. Cut into squares and serve.

Shawn Randazzo

The Chicken-Bacon-Ranch Detroit-Style

Makes 2 (10 by 14-inch) pizzas or 3 (9 by 9-inch) pan pizzas

Detroit–style pizza is having its moment after sixty years of being such a secret that many folks from Detroit didn't even know such a thing existed. As it turns out, they did know, but they just called it pizza, as these rectangular and square pies, baked in blue steel pans, were scattered all around the Detroit metropolitan area, all tracing their lineage back to Gus Guerra at Buddy's Rendezvous in 1946. Later, after Gus sold his interest in the Rendezvous (now simply known as Buddy's), he moved over to start the Cloverleaf Bar and Restaurant.

In 1995, a young delivery boy for Cloverleaf named Shawn Randazzo decided that this pizza was his calling. He immersed himself in the business and eventually bought one of the Cloverleaf branch operations and made it his own, eventually calling it the Detroit Style Pizza Company. By 2012, he had won his first of two world championships with his updated version of the classic Detroit square pie. Along with a few other key players, he perfected and elevated this style with its buttery, crunchy under-crust, fried-crisp edges, and a creamy, cheesy, focaccia-like interior, and brought it into the mainstream. Shawn even started a service within his company to provide pans, tools, and ingredients for other operators and home cooks. It's safe to say that, along with Jeff Smokevitch (see page 120), Shawn has been the modern godfather of the Detroit–style pizza boom.

Here's the hard part for me to write: When I interviewed Shawn on *Pizza Talk* during the summer of 2020, he told the viewers about his battle with Stage 4 glioblastoma brain cancer and how he had been battling back, returning to work and guiding his company through the COVID challenges. In that episode, he shared his classical method (part of his personal mission was to preserve the lineage of techniques going all the way back to Gus Guerra and his immediate disciples). A few weeks after his episode aired, the cancer came back with a vengeance and quickly took Shawn, only forty-four years old, from his wife, Keri, and their beautiful family, and all of us. The pizza community went into a deep state of mourning—we all miss his talent, delightful personality, and generous spirit. Rest in peace, Shawn.

This pizza is my tribute version based on the one he shared with me for the book, with the addition of my own embedded cheese technique, which Shawn told me he really wanted to try. Here it is, Shawn, just for you.

Pan Pizza Dough (page 28)

Butter paste (page 11)

6 ounces (170 grams) white cheddar cheese (mild or medium sharp), shredded (about 3 cups)

12 ounces (340 grams) whole milk mozzarella, cut into ½-inch cubes (about 6 cups)

6 ounces (170 grams) brick, fontina, Muenster, or provolone cheese, cut into ½-inch cubes (about 3 cups)

1 teaspoon granulated garlic

¼ teaspoon paprika (optional)

¼ teaspoon salt

⅛ teaspoon black pepper

16 ounces (454 grams) boneless chicken breast

12 ounces (340 grams) Applewood or Hickory smoked bacon

1 medium red onion

Susan's Ranch Dressing (page 96)

¼ cup chopped Italian parsley (for garnish)

Five hours before baking the pizzas, remove the dough from the refrigerator. Divide it into the desired weights based on the size of your pans (see chart on page 12). Grease the inside of the pans, including the side walls, with the butter paste. Transfer the dough pieces to the greased pans, rub the top with olive oil, and begin dimpling the dough. Rub the surface with more olive oil and cover the pans with a large plastic bag or plastic wrap. Let the dough rest at room temperature for 20 minutes and dimple it again, then set it aside to rest for another 20 minutes. It will take 3 or 4 dimpling cycles at 20-minute intervals for the dough to fully cover the surface of the pans.

Once the pans are evenly filled by the dough, distribute the cheddar cheese around the perimeter against the inside walls, creating a collar of shredded cheese. Mix together the cubed cheeses and divide the mixture evenly into 2 bowls. Use one of the bowls and distribute half or a third of the cheese cubes (depending on the size of the pans) evenly over the surface of the pizzas. Cover the pans with plastic wrap and rest at room temperature for 4 hours. The dough will bubble and rise and embed the cheese cubes and will be very soft and fragile, so handle it gently.

While the dough is rising, make a spice rub by whisking together the garlic, salt, pepper, and paprika. Rub the chicken breast with olive oil and roll it in the spice rub to coat it completely. Line a small baking pan with baking parchment and lightly mist the parchment with oil spray. Transfer the chicken breast to the pan. Preheat the oven to 375°F.

While the oven is preheating, line 1 or 2 sheet pans with baking parchment. Lay out the bacon strips on the pans. Place the bacon pan(s) and the chicken breast pan into the oven on separate racks, with the chicken on the upper-middle one and the bacon on the lower-middle rack or racks. Bake for 10 minutes, then rotate 180 degrees and continue baking for 5 to 10 additional minutes, until the bacon browns and crisps, and the chicken is firm and springy to the touch. Remove the pans from the oven and drain off any bacon fat into a heat-resistant bowl, saving the fat for the next step. Let the bacon and chicken cool for 30 minutes at room temperature. While the bacon and chicken are cooling, slice the onion into thin strips, julienne-style, 2 to 3 inches long and ⅛-inch wide.

Stack the bacon strips and chop them into bite-size bits, about ½ inch wide and long. Slice the cooled chicken breast into ¾-inch cubes or pieces. Combine the bacon and chicken pieces in a bowl and add enough of the bacon fat to coat everything (about 2 tablespoons). Add the sliced onions and toss the mixture to evenly distribute the ingredients. Cover the bowl with plastic wrap and place it in the refrigerator to chill and form clumps.

An hour before baking the pizzas, preheat the oven to 475°F. Add the remaining cheese cubes to cover the surface and perimeter of the dough. Evenly distribute scoops of the bacon, chicken, and onion mixture, in small clumps, over the cheese. Place the pan on the middle rack and bake for 9 minutes. Rotate 180 degrees and continue baking for an additional 6 to 9 minutes, until the dough is fully baked and springy to the touch, golden brown on top and caramelized to a medium golden brown on the underside, with a very caramelized crispy cheese edge (the *frico*). Transfer the pan(s) from the oven to a heat-resistant surface, such as the stovetop.

Use a metal bench or pastry blade to trace around the perimeter of the pizza, separating it from the pan. Use the bench blade or a metal spatula to lift and guide the pizza from the pan onto a cutting board. Drizzle the ranch dressing in streaks over the top of the pizza. Garnish with a small amount of chopped parsley. Slice into squares and serve.

Laura Meyer

Pan-Style Siciliano with Bresaola, Lemons, and Capers

Makes 1 (12 by 18-inch) pan pizza

Laura Meyer is one of the many protégés of Tony Gemignani, and she continues to work with and for Tony as part of his core team. More importantly (in my opinion), Laura is also now a lead instructor at Tony Gemignani's International School of Pizza in the North Beach neighborhood of San Francisco. The school is an American branch of the Scuola Italiana Pizzaioli. At their school, Laura and Tony certify future pizzeria operators and enthusiasts, passing on their knowledge of all styles of pizza to the next generation. At the same time, Laura has competed at the highest level and was the first female gold medal winner at the World Pizza Championship in Parma, Italy. She continues to create inventive pizzas drawn from her childhood food memories, instilled by her Mexican mother and onetime professional chef dad. "We ate really good food at home, usually cooked by my dad," she said about her childhood in Northern California and how it shaped her passion for cooking.

This tribute pizza, based on Laura's original concept, captures the spirit and bright flavors of Italian sliced beef (bresaola) with lemon and capers, on a focaccia-like Sicilian–style dough featuring sprouted grains. What I especially like about this "Moss" (for mozzarella) and Sauce Sicilian pie is how it showcases the convergence of tradition with a very contemporary understanding of pizza evolution and dough development.

Pan Pizza Dough, sourdough version, with 5 percent sprouted whole-wheat flour or sprouted mash (page 28), made at least a day ahead (see note)

4 tablespoons olive oil, divided

6 ounces (170 grams) thinly sliced bresaola (see sidebar)

¼ cup capers

1 lemon, preferably organic, seeded and sliced paper-thin

¾ cup Crushed Tomato Pizza Sauce (page 42)

3 ounces (85 grams) whole milk mozzarella, shredded (about ¾ cup)

3 ounces (85 grams) part-skim milk mozzarella, shredded (about ¾ cup)

1 cup grated Parmesan or Romano cheese

What is bresaola?

It's dry-salted, herb and spice-cured, thinly sliced lean meat, typically made with top round beef, but it can also be from pork or game meats. It's associated with the northern Lombardy region of Italy, but now, as with so many other regionally associated products, it can be found almost anywhere in the world. Your local butcher or specialty meat shop is likely to have it, and you can have them slice it paper-thin for you.

Six hours before baking, remove the dough from the refrigerator. Line a 12 by 18-inch sheet pan with baking parchment or a silicone baking mat and use 2 tablespoons of the olive oil to generously oil the surface, as well as the inside walls. Transfer the dough to the pan, rub the top with oil from the pan, and begin dimpling it. Rub the surface with more oil and cover the pan with plastic wrap. Let the dough rest at room temperature for 20 minutes, then dimple it again, cover it, and set it aside to rest for 20 minutes. It will take 3 or 4 dimpling cycles at 20-minute intervals for the dough to cover the full surface of the pan. Once the dough has evenly filled the pan, rub or brush the top with more oil, cover it and proof at room temperature for 4 hours. The dough will bubble and rise and be very soft and fragile, so handle the pan gently.

Preheat the oven to 475°F. Place the pan on the middle rack and bake for 10 minutes, then rotate 180 degrees and continue baking for an additional 6 to 8 minutes, until the dough is fully baked and springy to the touch, golden brown on top and caramelized to a light to medium golden brown on the underside. Remove the pan from the oven and set it aside to cool.

While the dough is baking, peel apart and place the slices of bresaola in a bowl and add the remaining olive oil, the capers, and the lemon slices, mixing gently to coat all the slices with the mixture.

When you're ready to bake the finished pizza, preheat the oven to 500°F. Spread the tomato sauce over the baked crust, leaving ½ inch around the perimeter uncovered. Evenly distribute the mozzarella over the sauce, again leaving a ½-inch border uncovered. Lay the slices of marinated bresaola, along with the lemon slices and capers, over the cheese. Place the pan on the middle rack and bake for 6 minutes, then rotate 180 degrees and bake for an additional 6 to 10 minutes, until the cheese begins to bubble and caramelize. Remove the pan from the oven and rest it on a heat-resistant surface, such as the stovetop.

Use a metal bench or pastry blade to trace around the perimeter of the pizza, separating it from the pan. Use the bench blade or a metal spatula to lift and guide the pizza from the pan onto a cutting board. If the parchment or silicone mat is still stuck to the underside, carefully lift the corner of the pizza and peel the paper or mat off. Garnish with the Parmesan. Let the pizza cool for 3 to 4 minutes, then cut it into squares and serve.

Note: This dough is a variation of the Pan Pizza Dough (page 28), but you can replace 5 percent of the white flour with sprouted whole-wheat flour, which is available at most supermarkets. Laura uses sprouted grain "mash" in her dough, because she has access to this product due to the proximity of Central Milling, which provides sprouted mashes made from a variety of grains to the baking community. Unless you want to make your own mash or have access to this mash, the sprouted wheat flour will work fine. I also advise you to use the "spiked" method (see page 13), in which you add a small amount of commercial yeast (1 teaspoon) to the dough to ensure a good rise in a timely manner. (If you are a sourdough purist and don't want to use commercial yeast, allow an extra hour or two for the various rising/proofing cycles.)

Focaccia, Roman, Stuffed, and Specialty Pies

Chicago-Style Stuffed Pizza with Italian Sausage, Onions, and Peppers

Makes 2 (9 or 10-inch) stuffed pizzas

We used to refer to Leo Spizzirri, the master instructor and co-founder (along with Anthony Iannone of the North American Pizza and Culinary Academy in Chicago), as, in his own words, "the greatest guy you never knew." That's mainly because Leo doesn't operate a pizza restaurant (though he certainly paid his dues working in the restaurants of others) and because much of his work is behind the scenes, consulting for large food service companies. But when I first met Leo at Pizza Expo a few years ago, I was struck by what a dynamic performer he was in front of the oven and an audience. In fact, he was working at four booths during the Expo, running between them in the mile-long convention hall on a very tight schedule, demonstrating everything from the many things you can do with a wood-fired oven to how to make dough, while also talking about his new school and making pizzas for a cheese company—he was clearly the hardest-working guy at the Expo, and yes, until then I never knew about him. But that weekend, I watched as he would start a demo with maybe six people in the audience and, before long, would draw a crowd of hundreds to watch him perform his magic.

So I arranged to interview him and, now that I do know him, discovered that he not only is indeed the greatest guy but is also one of the most knowledgeable people in the pizza business.

Leo spent a lot of his formative years working in his native Chicago for some of the great deep-dish and stuffed pizza companies in the country and, over time, perfected his own version (you can see him in action making this pie on YouTube or in his *Pizza Talk* interview with me). The following tribute version requires only a couple of 9 or 10-inch cake pans with 2-inch or higher sidewalls, and you'll be in business. When you cut your first slice, note the long "cheese pull" as it stretches from the pan. This is one of the perks of this pie and can lead to bonus bragging rights contests. See how far you can pull it before the cheese strand snaps. Then watch Leo's video . . .

New York Pizza Dough (page 30), made at least a day ahead, with the following modifications: reduce the water by 1 ounce (28 grams) and replace the olive oil with an equal amount of lard (optional)

Crushed Tomato Pizza Sauce (page 42)

6 ounces (170 grams) canned tomato paste

Salt and pepper

2 tablespoons unsalted butter

2 teaspoons olive oil

¾ tablespoon bread or all-purpose flour

4 ounces (113 grams) Parmesan cheese, grated (about 2 cups)

16 ounces (454 grams) Italian sausage (loose), either sweet or spicy

20 ounces (567 grams) whole milk mozzarella, shredded

20 ounces (567 grams) low-fat mozzarella, shredded

1 green bell pepper, seeded and julienned

1 medium white or yellow onion, julienned

Three hours before baking, remove the dough from the refrigerator and divide it into 2 large (9.5-ounce/269-gram) pieces and 2 smaller (8-ounce/227-gram) pieces. Lightly mist 2 sheet pans with vegetable oil spray. Form the dough pieces into tight dough balls and place them on the pans, then mist the top of the dough balls with the oil spray and cover the pans loosely with plastic wrap. Set aside to proof at room temperature for about 3 hours.

While the dough is rising, whisk together the sauce and tomato paste, then add salt and pepper to taste. Refrigerate.

Forty-five minutes before baking, preheat the oven to 475°F. No baking stone is required.

Melt the butter over low heat, removing it from the heat as soon as it melts, then add the olive oil. Let the mixture cool until it's lukewarm, then whisk in the flour to make a flour paste. Use a pastry brush to brush the bottom and the inside walls of the cake pans with the flour paste. Pour ½ cup of the Parmesan cheese into each pan, tilting and turning the pans so the cheese coats the bottom and sidewalls.

Rub ½ teaspoon of olive oil on the work surface to make an oil slick 14 to 15 inches in diameter. With a rolling pin, roll out one of the larger dough balls, working from the center to the perimeter, to form a circle. If the dough resists or shrinks back, let it rest for about 2 minutes, then lift it and lay it back on the work surface. Continue to evenly roll it out into a circle about 14 inches in diameter and ¼-inch thick, like a pie dough. Gently lift the dough and drape it over one of the pans. Carefully tuck the dough into the pan, covering the entire inner surface, including the sidewalls and corners. Pat the dough to remove any air bubbles. The dough should stick to the sidewalls and extend slightly over the edges of the pans.

Use the rolling pin to roll over the top of the pan, cutting off the excess dough. Add the scraps to another dough if you'd like. Repeat this process with the other large dough ball in the second pan, or save one large and one small dough ball for another time by placing them in a resealable freezer bag and returning them to the refrigerator.

Pinch off pieces of the sausage and cover the bottom of the pans with it. Distribute half of the mozzarella (10 ounces/284 grams of each type) into each pan. Set the pans aside and roll out the smaller dough balls as you did earlier with the larger balls, rolling them to 10 inches in diameter. Lift and drape the dough over the cheese and into the pan, tucking it in around the perimeter of the filling to seal the pie. Use a paring knife or pinch with your fingers to make 6 vent holes to allow steam to escape. Ladle in enough of the tomato sauce to generously cover the surface of the top crust, about ¼-inch thick. Distribute the green peppers and onions over the surface, followed by a generous sprinkling of the Parmesan cheese.

Bake for 15 minutes on the middle oven rack, then rotate 180 degrees and continue baking for 10 to 15 minutes, until the sauce is bubbling away and the Parmesan cheese and the dough around the edge are a rich golden brown. Transfer the pan from the oven to a heat-resistant surface, such as the stovetop. Allow 3 to 5 minutes for cooling, then use a metal spatula or knife to trace around the crust, releasing it from the pan. Use the metal spatula to lift and slide the pizza from the pan onto a cutting board. Cut into wedges and serve.

Note: For a vegetarian option, replace the sausage with 2 cups of uncooked baby spinach (per pie), and a sprinkling of nutmeg, salt, and pepper. One cup of sliced white or brown mushrooms may also be added before the mozzarella.

John Arena

Fried "Pantaloon" Calzone

Makes 4 large calzones

Probably the most frequently featured pizza master on *Pizza Quest* and on *Pizza Talk*, John Arena, the co-founder and head pizzaiolo of Metro Pizza in Las Vegas, is the son of a "pizza guy" and is proud to be known as "the other pizza guy" (his ninety-year-old dad still works shifts in the pizzeria). I often refer to him as the Yoda of the pizza world, because he serves as a mentor and teacher to many and is full of wise, pithy sayings ("The two most important tools for a pizza maker are these," he says, holding up his hands, which has now become the rallying image of the These Hands movement). Importantly, John follows his own never-ending pizza quest, tirelessly attending conferences and festivals around the world and bringing that knowledge back to share with the American pizza community at Pizza Expo and other gatherings. In addition to overseeing a number of Metro Pizza locations in Las Vegas, John teaches courses on the business of pizza as well as its history. There are a lot of wonderful people in the extended pizza community, but I think it's safe to say John Arena is probably the most beloved of them all.

During our calzone episode on *Pizza Talk*, John showed us his deep-fried version. It is spectacular to behold, puffing up like a pair of clown's pants (*calzone* translates to "stocking" or "trousers," thus ballooning out like pantaloons). I hope you'll check it out on our site; it's a simple master class and will likely inspire you to want to immediately make one yourself. In the meantime, here's my tribute version of John's classic. Both versions, I think, are pretty spectacular.

New York Pizza Dough (page 30)

6 ounces (170 grams) fresh mozzarella (fior di latte), shredded (about 1 cup), or 4 ounces (113 grams) whole milk mozzarella

32 ounces (907 grams or 1 quart) ricotta cheese

1.5 ounces (43 grams) Pecorino Romano or Parmesan cheese, grated (about ½ cup), divided

2 ounces (57 grams) deli ham, diced into small cubes

½ cup minced Italian parsley, divided

½ teaspoon kosher salt

¼ teaspoon black pepper

1 quart frying oil, such as corn, peanut, or canola

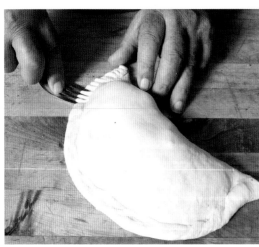

Two hours before frying the calzones, remove the dough from the refrigerator. Divide it into 4 (9-ounce/255-gram) pieces. Lightly mist a sheet pan with oil spray. Form each dough piece into a tight dough ball, then place them on the pan. Mist them with oil spray and cover the pan loosely with plastic wrap. Set the dough aside at room temperature to proof.

While the dough is rising, prepare the filling: Shred the mozzarella or cut it into bite-size pieces and place them in a mixing bowl, if necessary. Mix together the ricotta, two-thirds of the grated Romano or Parmesan (save the rest for garnish), the diced ham, two-thirds of the minced parsley (save the rest for garnish), and the salt and pepper. Add this mixture to the mozzarella cheese. Use a whisk to whip the mixture together for about 20 seconds to fully distribute the ingredients and to fluff it up slightly. Refrigerate.

When it's time to fry the calzone, pour the oil into a pot that's at least 12 inches in diameter and heat it over medium-high heat, bringing it to 350°F. While the oil is heating, form the calzones. You can make and fry one at a time, or form all 4 calzones and fry them one after another (any unused dough balls can be returned to the refrigerator for up to 4 days). Lightly rub ½ teaspoon of vegetable or olive oil on the work surface, forming an oil slick about 15 inches in diameter. Place a dough ball in the center of the slick and press with your palm to flatten it. Use your fingertips to extend the diameter, dimpling the dough from the center to the outer edges. When the dough resists spreading or springs back, let it rest for 30 to 60 seconds to relax the gluten (or move on to another dough ball), then resume pressing it out into a wider circle. Continue this dimpling process until the dough is 12 inches in diameter. If needed, lift it and re-oil the work surface, then complete the pressing.

Spoon one-quarter of the cheese mixture onto the half of the dough circle farthest from you, gently spreading it with the back of the spoon to 1 inch from the outer edge of its hemisphere, leaving the other half uncovered. Fold the uncovered section over the filled half to enclose the filling, matching up the edges of the top and lower halves. Dip your fingers in water and crimp the top and bottom together by pressing and sealing the outer edge. The calzone will now have a half-moon shape and is ready for the fryer. Do not cut a slit in the top of the calzone, and be sure the entire outer rim is sealed tight. You can press out and fill the other pieces or simply fry the piece at hand.

Using a large cooking spoon or a skimmer or "spider," carefully lower the filled calzone into the oil. It will bob to the surface almost immediately. Use a large spoon to ladle hot oil over the top for at least 1 minute. Then gently flip the calzone over and continue to spoon hot oil over the exposed top. After another minute, flip it over again. Continue frying in this manner until the dough is a rich, golden brown on both sides. The calzone will expand greatly in size due to the internal steam generated by the hot oil, and it will start to form the "pantaloon" shape it's named for.

Place a cooling rack over a sheet pan or paper towels to catch oil drips. Use the skimmer or spider or a slotted spoon to lift the calzone out of the oil and place it on the rack. Immediately sprinkle some of the grated cheese over the top, followed by a sprinkle of minced parsley. Allow 3 minutes for cooling, then serve the calzone on a plate with a knife and fork, or wrap it in butcher or deli paper to be eaten by hand.

Tony Gemignani

Cast-Iron Tomato and Mint Pizza

Makes 4 pizzas in 9-inch cast-iron pans

The name Tony Gemignani keeps coming up throughout this book, and with good reason. After all, as I said on page 79, he is "the Mozart of pizza" and has emerged as the most influential operator and educator (a rare combination) in the pizza universe. In this contribution, he tackles the growing interest in cast-iron pan pizzas, which is a kind of hybrid of Chicago deep pan (think Pequod's, not Uno) and Detroit styles, but with the added challenge of transmitting the heat through the thick cast-iron barrier of the pan to crisp the under-crust before the top ingredients get too dark. The added baking time, along with the application of sauce and tomato slices and the addition of the embedded cheese technique (my contribution to this tribute pizza, see page 124), all dramatically come together to create this beautiful, colorful, layered, and crispy-edged pizza.

Pan Pizza Dough (page 28), made at least a day ahead

Butter paste (page 11)

8 ounces (227 grams) mild or medium sharp cheddar cheese, cut into ¼-inch cubes (about 2 cups)

8 ounces (227 grams) low-moisture, full-fat mozzarella, cut into ¼-inch cubes (about 2 cups)

8 ounces (227 grams) provolone or fontina cheese, cut into ¼-inch cubes (about 2 cups)

Crushed Tomato Pizza Sauce (page 42)

4 green serrano or jalapeño peppers

4 cups Sungold, cherry, or grape tomatoes, halved

2 large or 4 medium ripe heirloom or Roma tomatoes

1 can cooked Gigante beans or other cooked white beans

2 tablespoons olive oil

Small bunch of fresh mint

1 cup water

1 cup granulated sugar

8 ounces (227 grams) fresh goat's milk cheese (such as chèvre)

Coarse or flake sea salt

Freshly ground black pepper

Five hours before making the pizzas, remove the dough from the refrigerator and divide it into 4 (9-ounce/255-gram) pieces, patted into a loose circle. Brush the inside of each cast-iron pan, including the walls, with 1½ tablespoons of the butter paste. With oiled hands, lift the dough and place it into the pan. (You can prepare as many pizzas at a time as you have pans and can bake 2 pans at a time in the oven, and you can also reserve extra dough pieces in an oiled freezer bag for later baking.) Use your fingertips to dimple the dough from the center to the outer edges. The dough will spring back, so cover each pan loosely with plastic wrap and set them aside to rest for 20 minutes. Then dimple the dough again with oiled fingertips from the center to the outer edges. Again, let the dough rest for 20 minutes and repeat the dimpling process. The dough should now cover the whole surface of the pan; if not, perform an additional 20-minute rest and dimpling cycle.

During the resting intervals, gather the cubed cheese pieces, keeping the cheddar cheese separate but combining the mozzarella and provolone in a single bowl.

Use one-quarter of the cubed cheddar cheese (about ½ cup) for each pizza and distribute the pieces around the perimeter of the dough, right up against the pan walls. Then take one-quarter of the provolone and one-quarter of the mozzarella cubes (about ½ cup) and distribute them over the entire surface of the dough. Cover loosely with plastic wrap and set aside to rise for 4 hours; the dough will become very soft and bubbly.

While the dough is rising, slice the chili peppers into ¼-inch thick rings, discarding the seeds as you slice. Halve the cherry tomatoes and place them in a bowl, then cover and refrigerate. Slice the large tomatoes into ¼-inch thick rounds and place them in a bowl, then cover and refrigerate. Drain the beans and place them in a bowl; add 1 tablespoon of olive oil and gently toss to coat, then refrigerate.

Wash the mint leaves and stems with cold water to remove any grit. Remove 2 clusters of mint to use as garnish. Bring the water and sugar to a boil in a saucepan, then turn off the heat and add the remaining mint (as a bunch, not chopped) to the hot syrup. Steep for 15 to 30 minutes. Drain the syrup into a bowl, pressing as much of the liquid from the mint as possible, then it set aside.

When it's time to bake the pizzas, preheat the oven to 500°F. Distribute the remaining cheese cubes evenly over the surface of the pizzas, including around the perimeter of the pan (the dough will deflate slightly from the cheese). Ladle or drizzle ½ cup of the tomato sauce over the cheese. Space one-quarter of the sliced tomatoes evenly over the surface of the dough. Bake for 9 minutes (you can bake 2 pans on different racks, or bake one at a time on the middle rack).

Rotate the pan(s) 180 degrees and also switch racks, then bake for an additional 8 to 11 minutes, until the cheese is melted and caramelized and turns a rich dark brown (almost but not quite burnt) around the rim of the pizza. Use a heavy-duty pot holder or baking mitt to carry the pan to the stovetop or other heat-resistant surface. Use a metal icing spatula to trace around the perimeter, between the dough and the pan, and use a flexible metal spatula to carefully lift the pizza onto a cutting board (or you can serve the pizza directly from the cast-iron pan).

For each pizza, distribute one-quarter of the uncooked cherry or grape tomato halves over the top. Lay one-quarter of the hot pepper rings around the perimeter of each pizza, then distribute one-quarter of the white beans over the surface of each. Drizzle some of the mint-flavored simple syrup over the pizza, then drop dollops of goat cheese on top. Garnish with coarse or flaky salt and ground pepper to taste. Slice into wedges or squares and serve.

Tarte Flambé, Two Ways

Makes 3 (12-ounce/340-gram) tarte flambés

Classic Alsatian flammekueche, or what the French call tarte flambé (the French and the Germans each lay claim to Alsace and its unique cultural hybrid, so they each prefer their own name for this wonderful pastry/pizza), keeps making comebacks on American menus every few years. It will never go out of fashion because it's so good, and it keeps getting rediscovered by succeeding generations. An onion, bacon, and cheese flatbread—it doesn't get much simpler than that, yet it is beloved by many. Not to mention, it is beautiful as well as delicious.

Two of our most talented American pizza makers, Leo Spizzirri and Brian Spangler (featured on pages 132 and 51), have each come up with their own fabulous versions, similar yet different—good examples of our homegrown love of tweaking the classics, which, of course, I am also doing by tweaking their tweaks for these tribute versions. And the tweaks go on . . .

Leo's Version: Coriander Cream, Bacon Lardons, Onions, and Gruyere

Coriander Cream, made at least a day ahead (recipe follows)

3 large or 4 medium onions (yellow or white), julienned

4 tablespoons (¼ cup) olive oil

½ teaspoon kosher salt

⅛ teaspoon ground white pepper

16 ounces (454 grams) thick sliced bacon, cut into 1½-inch pieces

Classic White Dough (page 26), made at least a day ahead

8 ounces (227 grams) Gruyere cheese, shredded (about 4 cups)

A day before making the tartes, sauté the sliced onions with the olive oil in a large skillet or pot over medium heat. Stir every few minutes to prevent the onions from browning, and continue cooking for about 10 minutes, or until the onions wilt and become translucent and just begin to turn a very light amber. Stir in the salt and pepper and remove the pan from the heat. Position a colander over a bowl to catch the liquid, then transfer the onions into it. Strain for about 15 minutes. Return the onion liquid to the pan and simmer it over medium-high heat until the juice reduces to a thick syrup, about 5 minutes. Pour the thickened syrup back over the onions, stir, cool, cover, and refrigerate.

Place the bacon pieces in a different skillet and cook them over medium heat, stirring to separate the pieces and to render the fat. Continue cooking until the bacon begins to brown, but not until it's crisp. Strain off the fat into a stainless steel bowl and save it for later use. Place the cut bacon "lardons" in a small bowl, cool, cover, and refrigerate.

Three hours before baking, remove the dough from the refrigerator and divide it into 3 (12-ounce/340-gram) pieces. Mist a sheet pan with oil spray and, with lightly oiled hands, form each piece into a tight ball. Place them evenly spaced down the center of the pan in a vertical line. As you lay each one on the pan, gently squeeze it to form it into an oblong torpedo across the pan, 3 to 4 inches long. Mist the dough with oil spray and loosely cover the pan with plastic wrap. Set aside at room temperature to proof for about 3 hours.

While the dough is rising, assemble your topping ingredients, including the bacon and onions. An hour before baking the tartes, place a baking stone or baking steel on the middle oven rack and preheat to 550°F. Warm up the bacon fat if it has solidified.

When it's time to bake, dust a wooden cutting board with flour for use as a loading peel. Gently dimple all 3 pieces of dough into longer oblongs, across the width of the pan, as you would for focaccia. Lift the first piece and transfer it to the floured cutting board, pointing end to end in the same direction as the length of the

board. Slide the dough back and forth to pick up enough flour to keep it from sticking, then lift it and dust underneath it again with more flour. Dip your fingers into the flour and begin dimpling the dough to form a longer and wider oblong. It should not extend longer than the length and width of the baking stone, and it should be evenly spread out across the surface, right up to the outer edge. If the dough springs back, let it rest for a minute or two to allow the gluten to relax, then continue dimpling. The final oblong should be about ¼-inch thick, 16 to 17 inches long and about 8 inches wide. Continually test to see that the dough can slide on the board when you jiggle the board; if it is stuck, use a pastry or bench blade to break the contact, then dust underneath again with flour.

Spread the coriander cream sauce over the surface, leaving a ½-inch border around the edge without sauce. Evenly distribute one-third of the onion mixture over the sauced surface, then one-third of the shredded Gruyere cheese, followed by one-third of the bacon lardons. Brush some of the melted bacon fat around the uncovered perimeter border, being careful not to get any on the board. Test that the dough still slides when the board is jiggled. If not, lift it with a metal pastry blade and dust underneath again with flour. Slide the tarte from the peel onto the baking stone by holding the two long ends of the board and sliding the dough off one of the sides so that it fits on the stone, jiggling the board back and forth in short vibrations for maximum control. The tarte should fit comfortably on the stone.

Bake for 4 minutes, then use a metal spatula or metal tongs to rotate 180 degrees. Continue baking for an additional 3 to 5 minutes, until the dough is golden brown around the edge and also underneath, the cheese is bubbly and browning, and the bacon is crisp. Transfer the tarte to a clean cutting board, cut it into 6 to 8 sections, and serve while you begin preparing the next tarte.

Coriander Cream

1 quart heavy cream

4 tablespoons yogurt or buttermilk

1½ teaspoons ground coriander seed

2 egg yolks

Whisk together the sour cream and yogurt or buttermilk in a glass or stainless steel bowl. Cover with plastic wrap and leave at room temperature for about 12 hours, until the cream thickens into a yogurt-like consistency. Whisk in the ground coriander seed and the egg yolks, then refrigerate until assembly.

Brian's Version: Portland-Style

16 ounces (454 grams/1 pint) heavy cream

2 tablespoons yogurt or buttermilk (or use commercial crème fraîche or sour cream in place of these first two ingredients)

½ teaspoon ground nutmeg

4 large onions (yellow or white), julienned

4 tablespoons olive oil

Kosher salt

White or black pepper

6 ounces (170 grams) speck or smoked prosciutto, sliced very thin (see notes)

Sourdough Pizza Dough (page 32) or Classic White Dough (page 26), made at least a day ahead

16 ounces (454 grams) fromage blanc or fresh goat cheese, mascarpone, Boursin, quark, or cream cheese (see notes)

One or two days before making the tartes, make crème fraîche by whisking together the cream and the yogurt or buttermilk in a glass or stainless steel bowl. Cover with plastic wrap and leave at room temperature for about 12 hours, or until the cream thickens into a yogurt-like consistency (or use commercial crème fraîche or sour cream). Whisk in the ground nutmeg and refrigerate.

Also 1 or 2 days in advance, in a mixing bowl, stir together the sliced onions and the olive oil. Preheat the oven to 375°F. Spread the sliced onions onto a 12 by 18-inch sheet pan and bake on the middle rack for 15 to 20 minutes, until the onions begin to sweat and wilt. Stir to evenly distribute them and to break up clumps, and continue baking for an additional 10 to 15 minutes, until they begin to turn light amber or light brown. Remove the pan from the oven and transfer the onions into a mixing bowl. Stir in ½ teaspoon of kosher salt and ¼ teaspoon of white or black pepper, then set aside. Once cooled, cover the bowl with plastic wrap and refrigerate.

Slice the speck or smoked prosciutto (or bacon) into strips, about 1½ inches long and ½ inch wide. Separate the strips and place them in a bowl, keeping them loosely separated. Cover with plastic wrap and refrigerate.

Three hours before baking the tartes, remove the dough from the refrigerator and divide it into 3 (12-ounce/340-gram) pieces. Mist a sheet pan with oil spray and, with lightly oiled hands, form each piece into a tight dough ball. Place the dough balls on the pan, spaced at least 3 inches apart. Mist the dough with oil spray and loosely cover the pan with plastic wrap. Set aside at room temperature to proof for about 3 hours.

While the dough is rising, assemble topping ingredients. Strain out any liquid from the onions and whisk it into the crème fraîche. Combine the crème fraîche and the fromage blanc (or goat cheese or cream cheese or quark) in the bowl of an electric mixer. With the whisk attachment, whip the cheese mixture together at low speed for 30 seconds, then increase to medium-high and whisk for 1 to 2 minutes to make a light and fluffy mixture (you can also whip it by hand with a whisk).

An hour before baking, place a baking stone or baking steel on the middle oven rack and preheat to 550°F, or as hot as it will allow. When it's time to bake, stretch a dough ball as if for a large pizza, to 12 to 14 inches in diameter (see page 18). You can also use a rolling pin, rolling from the center to the outer edge in all directions.

Dust a wooden pizza peel or wooden cutting board with enough flour to prevent sticking, then lay the stretched dough on the peel or board. Jiggle the peel to ensure the dough isn't sticking. Use an icing spatula or the back of a tablespoon to spread one-third of the crème fraîche and cream cheese mixture over the surface, leaving a rim of only ¼-inch around the edge uncovered. Distribute one-third of the onion strips over the surface, followed by one-third of the speck strips. Check again that the dough is still able to slide on the peel. If not, use a metal spatula to lift it, and dust more flour underneath as needed.

Slide the tarte onto the baking stone or steel and bake for 4 minutes. Rotate 180 degrees and continue baking for an additional 2 to 4 minutes, until the edges of the crust, as well as the underside, are golden brown. The onions will also become more caramelized, and the speck will crisp slightly. Transfer the tarte to a cutting board and cut into squares or diamonds and serve while you prepare the next tarte.

Notes: Fromage blanc is a soft, spreadable cheese, thicker than yogurt, similar to crème fraîche or mascarpone but made with milk instead of cream. Quark is a similar German version, and you can substitute Boursin if you can't find fromage blanc at your cheese store. You can also just double up on the crème fraîche, or mascarpone or fresh goat's milk cheese, such as chèvre.

Speck is a cured and smoked ham originally made in the border area of southern Germany and northern Italy, and it's best described as akin to smoked prosciutto (though no one who makes it will agree to that description). You can also replace it in the recipe with bacon.

Nicky Giusto

Focaccia Slab on Sprouted Grain Crust with Asparagus and Lemon Ricotta

Makes 1 (12 by 18-inch) pan

I've known the Giusto family for over thirty years, ever since I lived in the Bay Area and owned Brother Juniper's Bakery in Santa Rosa. Back then, Nicky Giusto was just an infant, but his uncle, Keith, was my flour guy, and his family's mill supplied my flour. Keith, though still relatively young, knew more about flour than anyone I'd ever met and, as I later learned, was not just a miller but a very accomplished baker. He became one of my main go-to guys whenever I had a question about the functionality of flour and sourdough starters. When I sold my bakery and moved to the East Coast to teach at Johnson & Wales University, I lost touch with the Giusto family until I ran into Keith a few years later at a bread bakers gathering and discovered that he had left the family business and opened his own bakery supply company, consolidated a few independent milling companies in Utah and, with some new partners, formed Central Milling. In addition, he brought back a family legacy, sprouted grain mash, from the days of Giusto Vita-Grain Sprouted Breads from the 1950s (a precursor to Ezekiel Bread). Equally important, Keith invited his now grown and college-educated nephew, Nicky, to join the company to help run the business side and then, serendipitously, discovered that Nicky was a natural-born baker who quickly got so good at it that he eventually became the captain of the Team USA Coupe du Monde du Boulangerie (aka the World Cup of Bread team) in 2016. He later became the head coach for the following team in 2020 (the event, like the World Cup of soccer, is held every four years).

I'm telling you this because Central Milling, and Nicky and Keith Giusto, have been teaching the bread and pizza community how to choose or blend the right flour for their bakeries and restaurants for a number of years, and one of the newest developments in the pizza world is the use of sprouted grain. You can see that Laura Meyer (page 127) uses a little in her pizza dough, and she knows Central Milling well, since they supply a special blend of flour for Tony Gemignani's restaurants (where Laura works and teaches). At the Central Milling pavilion at Pizza Expo, I tasted one of Nicky's creations—a focaccia slab, he called it—made with sprouted ancient wheat (khorasan, in this instance) and really loved it. So when he appeared on *Pizza Talk*, I asked him if we could include it in this book, and he gave me all the information I needed to create this tribute version that anyone can bake at home. You'll notice that I offer the option of using sprouted wheat flour instead of sprouted mash, because it's difficult to source the mash unless you're a customer of Central Milling (or want to make it yourself), whereas sprouted wheat flour is readily available at most supermarkets. For those interested in doing more baking with sprouted grains, I wrote extensively about in an earlier book, *Bread Revolution*, where you can even learn how to make your own sprouted grain mash.

In the meantime, enjoy this wonderful, open-holed focaccia, and feel free to substitute your own favorite toppings, though I think Nicky's topping concept is quite special.

Pan Pizza Dough (recipe follows)

8 fresh, young (thin) asparagus spears

1 medium onion, julienned

3 large cloves garlic, sliced thin (not chopped)

2 tablespoons olive oil

4 tablespoons lemon juice, divided

½ teaspoon kosher salt

¼ teaspoon ground black pepper

1 cup ricotta cheese

1 tablespoon minced fresh thyme, oregano, parsley, or marjoram (or any combination)

The dough can be baked either directly on a baking stone or in a pan. If baking in a pan, remove the dough from the refrigerator 5 hours before baking. Line a 12 by 18-inch sheet pan with baking parchment or a silicone baking mat and generously oil the surface as well as the inside walls with 1½ tablespoons of olive oil. Transfer the dough into the oiled pan and begin dimpling it. Rub the surface with more olive oil and cover the pan with a large plastic bag or plastic wrap. Let the dough rest at room temperature for 20 minutes, then dimple it again and set it aside to rest. It will take 3 or 4 dimpling cycles at 20-minute intervals for the dough to cover the full surface of the pan. Once the pan is evenly covered by the dough, brush or spray olive oil on the surface of the dough, cover it with plastic wrap, and proof at room temperature for 4 hours. The dough will bubble and rise and be very soft and fragile, so handle it gently. (For baking the focaccia as a "slab" style, see instructions on page 151.)

While the dough is rising, cut off any woody sections from the bottoms of the asparagus spears. Slice the spears in half lengthwise, then slice each of the lengths into 2-inch pieces. In a mixing bowl, mix together the asparagus, onion, and garlic. Add the olive oil and 2 tablespoons of the lemon juice, reserving the remaining juice for the ricotta cream. Add the salt and pepper and toss to coat. Cover the bowl and refrigerate.

Forty-five minutes before baking, preheat the oven to 500°F. (If baking "slab" style on a stone or baking steel, preheat the stone or steel on the middle rack for an hour). Evenly distribute the asparagus mixture over the surface of the dough, drizzle any remaining oil or juice from the bowl over the asparagus mixture, and place the pan on the middle rack. Bake for 10 minutes, then rotate and continue baking for 9 to 12 minutes, until the dough is fully baked and springy to the touch, golden brown on top and caramelized to a medium golden brown on the underside. While the focaccia is baking, whisk together the ricotta cheese with the fresh herbs and the remaining lemon juice until it is slightly fluffy. Add salt and pepper to taste.

Remove the pan from the oven and set it on a heat-resistant surface, such as the stovetop. Use a metal spatula or bench blade to trace around the perimeter of the focaccia, releasing it from the pan. Use the bench blade or spatula to gently transfer the focaccia from the pan onto a cutting board. Spoon dollops of the ricotta cream, evenly spaced, over the surface and garnish with the herbs. Let the focaccia cool for at least 5 minutes before slicing it into 15 to 24 squares (3 by 5 inches or 4 by 6 inches) and serving.

**Baking the Focaccia "Slab-Style"

It's always tricky transferring a sticky dough directly onto a baking stone when it's not contained inside a baking pan. Here's a method that will allow you to bake the focaccia in a more free-form manner without causing it to stick to the peel when you attempt to slide it into the oven:

Lightly dust the back of a dry sheet pan, or the surface of a large cutting board, with flour. Then lay a sheet of baking parchment, cut to fit, on the back of the pan or on the board. Rub the baking parchment with 1 tablespoon of olive oil, covering the whole surface, then transfer the dough from the bowl to the middle of the parchment. Dip your fingers in olive oil and begin dimpling the dough as described in the pan version, including 20-minute resting intervals, and extend the dough into an oblong shape that covers most of the parchment but not to the corners or the edge. Leave an uncovered border of parchment around the perimeter of at least ¾ inch.

Instead of the long rise described for the pan version, preheat the oven for 1 hour as soon as the dimpling has been accomplished. Prepare all the toppings and top the focaccia as described for the pan version. Slide the focaccia, parchment and all, from the pan or board directly onto the baking stone/steel.

Note: Depending on the configuration of your oven, if the stone is horizontally placed, you'll have to slice the focaccia off the long side of the pan or board rather than short side, as you would for a vertically placed stone. Be sure to land the parchment fully on the stone or steel, not overhanging.

Bake for 10 minutes, then slide a metal spatula or peel under the parchment and rotate the focaccia 180 degrees for a more even bake. Bake an additional 7 to 10 minutes, until the focaccia is golden brown. Transfer the focaccia slab to a cutting board, lift one of the corners, and peel off and discard the parchment. Garnish and serve as described in the recipe.

Pan Pizza Dough (page 28), with the following substitutions:

18 ounces (510 grams) unbleached bread flour (4 cups)

3 ounces (85 grams) sprouted wheat flour or sprouted wheat mash (⅔ cup)

0.42 ounces (12 grams) kosher salt (1½ teaspoons)

0.11 ounces (3 grams) instant yeast (1 teaspoon)

18 ounces (510 grams) water (room temperature, 68° to 72°F)

1 ounce (28 grams) olive oil

Follow the procedure on page 28, making the dough at least a day ahead (or up to 3 days).

Note: This is a very wet, sticky dough, though it will get firmer after the stretch-and-folds and also after it ferments overnight in the refrigerator.

Double-Stuffed Roman-Style Pizza

(Pizza alla Scarala Napoletana a Chiava Romana)

Makes 24 servings

According to its creator, Massimiliano Saieva (Mas, for short), founder of the Roman Pizza Academy, here's what this double-crusted Roman–style pizza is really called: *Pizza alla Scarala Napoletana a Chiava Romana*— that is, Escarole Neapolitan Focaccia, Roman Version. Boy, that's a lot of references: Neapolitan (Naples), Roman, focaccia (which is Ligurian, a whole different region of Italy!). But here's the bottom line: it's a Christmas pizza! Here's what he has to say about it:

> This double-stuffed pizza is two layers, with the ingredients inside. It is my tribute to the two Italian emblematic pizza cities, Napoli and Roma. This is an example of a stuffed double pizza Bianca, with ricotta cheese and buffalo mozzarella, and with spicy sautéed escarole or spinach, and Gaeta olives.

As far as its history is concerned, as for many typical Neapolitan dishes—even for the escarole pizza—it was born in the period of poverty. During the Christmas holidays, the women who lived in the Neapolitan lowlands got busy preparing what at the time was called "pizza with jeta." The escarole was, in fact, too expensive for the masses, so it was replaced with chard, and the dough was fried. Slowly, then, the habit of making endive pizza in the oven took hold. So during the Christmas period, the escarole pizza became the symbol of a party that the Neapolitans fully love. And it can be served either hot or cold.

At the Roman Pizza Academy in Miami, Florida, Saieva is training a whole new generation of bakers how to make this unique, incredibly delicious Roman–style pizza. My tribute version is less stringent than Mas's, modified to use everyday equipment and designed for home cooks, but it will get you close. However, to see his beautiful creations, check out his videos on YouTube and social media. This category is inevitably destined to become huge as more people experience it.

Double-size batch Pan Pizza Dough (page 28), made at least a day ahead

½ cup pine nuts

1 large head (or 2 small heads) escarole, or an equal amount of kale, arugula, frisée, endive, or spinach (about 8 cups), chopped

¼ cup capers

¼ cup olive oil

¾ cup sliced black olives

1 cup raisins, soaked in 1 cup room temperature water overnight

½ teaspoon kosher salt

¼ teaspoon ground black pepper

2 cups ricotta cheese

8 ounces (227 grams) fresh buffalo mozzarella or burrata, cut into about 12 pieces (you can substitute fior di latte if necessary)

Four hours before baking, remove the dough from the refrigerator. Line 2 (12 by 18-inch) sheet pans with baking parchment or silicone baking pads. Oil each pan, including the sidewalls, with 1 tablespoon of olive oil. Divide the dough into 2 (38-ounce/1.08-kilogram) pieces and place a piece in the center of each pan. With oiled hands and fingertips, press and dimple the dough so that it fills about 60 percent of the pans. Repeat this every 20 minutes until the dough evenly fills the pans; this should take about an hour. Brush the tops of the doughs with olive oil and loosely cover the pans with plastic wrap. Set the pans aside at room temperature to proof for 3 hours, or until the dough is soft and bubbly and has risen to fill the pans to the rim.

While the dough is rising, toast the pine nuts in a dry pan over medium heat for 4 to 6 minutes, until light brown and fragrant. Transfer the nuts from the pan to a bowl and set it aside to cool. Wash, dry thoroughly, and coarsely chop the greens. Heat a wok or large pot or frying pan over high heat and add the olive oil. Add the greens and sauté until they become limp and turn bright green. Turn off the heat and add the pine nuts, olives, and soaked raisins (the raisins will have absorbed all their soaking liquid). Stir in the salt and pepper and set this mixture aside to cool.

Set up 2 racks in the upper middle and lower middle sections of the oven (no baking stone required), then preheat to 500°F. Bake both pans of dough for 8 minutes, then rotate 180 degrees and swap shelves to continue baking for 8 to 10 additional minutes, until the tops are golden brown and the underside of each is a light to medium brown. Remove the pans from the oven to a heat-resistant surface, such as the stovetop. Leave the oven on. Use a pastry or bench blade or a metal spatula to trace around the perimeter of one of the pans to break any contact between the pan and the crust. Then use the bench blade to guide the crust from the pan onto a cutting board. Leave the other crust in its pan.

Use tongs or a slotted spoon to distribute the cooked greens filling over the surface of the crust still in the pan; discard any liquid from the greens (or save it to add to soup; it's delicious and full of minerals). Distribute the ricotta over the greens, followed by the buffalo mozzarella or burrata.

Set the second dough on top of the filling and return the now 2-layered pizza to the hot oven for 5 to 7 minutes, until the cheese melts. Remove from the oven and brush the top with olive oil. Use a pastry blade or metal spatula to remove and transfer the entire pizza to a cutting board. Cut into 12 (4 by 3-inch) rectangles, then cut each rectangle into 2 triangles and serve.

Rita Bella Pizza al Taglia

Makes 1 (12 by 18-inch) pizza

Mia Marco's Pizza is a very popular and beloved food truck operating in the border area between Selma and Schertz, Texas, just outside San Antonio. Derek Sanchez, one of the founding partners, is not only an award-winning pizzaiolo, but also a practicing doctor specializing in physical therapy. His pie featured here brings together sweet and savory flavors in much the same manner as (don't kill the messenger) pineapple and ham on a so-called Hawaiian pizza. In this instance, though, it's apricots and bacon that come together to accomplish a delightful synergy that bursts in your mouth with intense flavor. Plus, it has an airy, crispy crust baked in what is called *al taglia* (in a pan, in the Roman pizza style). Between the flavors of the topping and texture of the crust, it's a total win-win.

Apricot preserves are one of the greatest of the jams, in my mind. Apricots seem to elevate everything they're used with, from hot buttered toast to glazes on proteins. At home, I mix it with homemade hot pepper, vinegar, and garlic mash to make a chutney-like condiment that makes a perfect dipping sauce for chicken wings and ribs. There's a lot more going on in this pizza than just apricots, but they're the secret ingredient that ties everything together and makes this pizza so memorable. I hope Mia and Marco (Derek's kids, who got to have a pizzeria named after them—how cool is that?) are collecting their own tasty food memories and will someday pay it forward, whether with apricots and bacon or something entirely new.

Pan Pizza Dough (page 28), made at least a day ahead

3 tablespoons butter paste (page 11)

16 ounces (454 grams) smoked black pepper bacon

12-ounce jar apricot preserves

1 tablespoon Tabasco or other hot pepper sauce (more if desired)

¾ cup pecan halves

6 ounces (170 grams) mozzarella di bufala

4 ounces (113 grams) whole milk (full fat) mozzarella, shredded (about 2 cups)

4 ounces (113 grams) fontina cheese, shredded (about 2 cups)

½ cup baby arugula

12 fresh basil leaves

1 tablespoon olive oil

8 dried apricots, sliced into slivers

4 ounces (113 grams) mascarpone cheese

2 ounces (57 grams) aged Parmesan, grated (about ½ cup)

Five hours before baking, remove the dough from the refrigerator. Line a 12 by 18-inch sheet pan with baking parchment or a silicone baking pad. Use the butter paste to generously grease the surface of the pan as well as the inside walls. Transfer the dough to the center of the greased pan and begin dimpling it. Rub the surface of the dough with more olive oil and cover the pan with a plastic wrap. Let the dough rest at room temperature for 20 minutes, then dimple the dough again and set it aside to rest. It will take 3 or 4 dimpling cycles at 20-minute intervals for the dough to cover the full surface of the pan. Once the pan is evenly filled by the dough, rub or mist it with olive oil, cover it, and proof at room temperature for 3 to 4 hours. The dough will bubble and rise to the top of the pan and will be very soft and fragile, so handle it gently.

While the dough is rising, preheat the oven to 375°F and lay out the strips of bacon on a sheet pan. Bake the bacon until it begins to brown but is not totally crisp. Remove the pan from the oven and set it on a heat-resistant surface, such as the stovetop. Drain the bacon fat and save it for use in other recipes (such as Tarte Flambé, page 143).

Place the apricot preserves in a saucepan and stir in the hot sauce. Slowly bring this to a simmer, then turn off the heat. Warm it later when the pizza is baking.

Toast the pecan halves in a dry skillet or pan, or lay them out on a sheet pan and bake at 350°F for about 8 minutes, until they fill the kitchen with the aroma of toasted nuts. Remove them from the heat and set them aside to cool. Drain the fresh mozzarella and slice it into ½-inch thick rounds. Place them in a bowl and add the shredded mozzarella and fontina. Toss or mix the cheeses together.

Preheat the oven to 475°F. Cover the surface of the dough with the cheese blend. Cut the bacon into 1-inch squares and distribute them evenly over the surface of the pizza. Place the pan on the middle rack. While the pizza is baking, wash and pat dry the arugula and basil leaves and place them in a bowl. Add the olive oil and toss to coat the leaves.

After 10 minutes of baking, rotate the pan and continue baking for 7 to 12 additional minutes, until the dough is fully baked and springy to the touch, the cheese is caramelized to a light to medium golden brown, and the underside of the crust is golden brown.

Remove the pan from the oven and set it on a heat-resistant surface, such as the stovetop. Use a metal spatula or pastry blade to trace around the perimeter of the pizza and carefully lift and slide the pizza onto a cutting board. (If the parchment sticks to the under-crust, peel it off after the transfer.) Immediately distribute the dried apricot slivers over the top of the pizza, into the melted cheese, then drizzle streaks of the spicy apricot glaze over the top. Place the pecan halves over the top and evenly space 12 (1-teaspoon) dollops of mascarpone cheese over the surface. Spread the arugula/basil mixture over the surface (it should garnish but not completely cover the toppings beneath) and finish by sprinkling the surface of the pizza with the Parmesan. Cut into squares and serve.

Note: If you want to get extra fancy, whip the mascarpone with a tablespoon or two of milk or cream to fluff it up, then pipe it onto the pizzas using a piping bag (or a freezer zip bag with a snip of the corner cut off) instead of spooning it on in dollops.

Poached Bosc Pear Schiacciata with Camembert, Stilton, Pecan, Maple Syrup, and Basil

Makes 2 (19-ounce/539-gram) schiacciata or 1 (12 by 18-inch) focaccia

In the small town of Athens, Ohio, John Gutekanst is kicking butt at Avalanche Pizza. A former white tablecloth chef, John brings a chef's sensibility, a respect for culinary history, and boundless creative energy to his work. He brings a non-stop avalanche of ideas to everything he does. John has so many out-of-the-box pizzas in his repertoire—many of which you can see on social media—that it inevitably gets your own wheels spinning.

In addition to running his own restaurant, John contributes regularly to pizza magazines and local philanthropic causes, and serves as an emcee and demo chef at all the pizza shows. The pizza featured here—he calls it schiacciata, which is the Tuscan equivalent of focaccia and literally translates to "squashed"— is an excellent example of John's creative imagination, bringing together the bold flavor combination of both Camembert and blue cheese (Stilton, no less) and pears, specifically Bosc pears, as he described this schiacciata to me:

> *This combination came about when my favorite fruit farmer, Neil Cherry of Cherry Orchards in Crooksville, Ohio, turned me on to the Bosc pear. I just love the sweet/sour taste of that pear and the smooth sourness of the baked Stilton. The pungent basil, along with the buttery chunks of pecan hidden underneath, and the finish of maple syrup add to the wow factor of this flatbread.*

John's version calls for baking it directly on the hearth, free-form, but for those who would like the safety net of baking it in a pan, I am also providing a focaccia version that's equally delicious, if not as visually spectacular.

Sourdough Pizza Dough (use the "mixed method" option, page 13, made at least 24 hours ahead, but preferably 48)

3 ripe but firm Bosc pears

Poaching liquid (recipe follows)

1 lemon, or 2 tablespoons lemon juice

8 ounces (227 grams) firm Camembert or Brie cheese

16 large basil leaves

8 ounces (227 grams) firm Stilton or other firm blue cheese

1 cup pecan halves

2 ounces (57 grams) maple syrup (4 tablespoons)

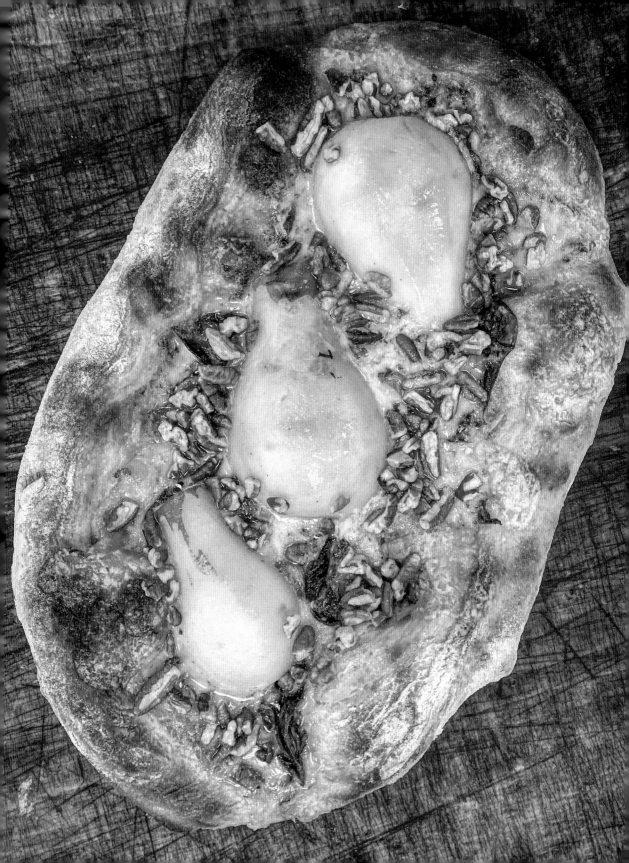

Four hours before baking, remove the dough from the refrigerator. Divide it in half for schiacciata, or leave it whole for the panned focaccia variation.

For the schiacciata version, mist a 12 by 18-inch sheet pan with oil spray, or rub it with olive oil. Form the dough into 2 equal-size dough balls (about 19 ounces each) and place them on the sheet pan. Mist the tops with the oil spray, loosely cover the pan with plastic wrap, and set it aside to proof at room temperature for 2 hours.

For the focaccia variation, line a 12 by 18-inch sheet pan with baking parchment or a silicone baking pad, then use 2 tablespoons of olive oil to grease the surface and inner walls of the pan. Begin the dimpling process, allowing 20 minutes between each dimpling cycle. Once the dough has evenly filled the pan (after about an hour), brush the surface with olive oil, cover the pan loosely with plastic wrap, and set aside to proof at room temperature for about 3 hours, or until the dough rises to the top of the pan.

While the dough is resting, prepare the poached pears as described on page 164, then refrigerate them. Toast the pecan halves in a dry skillet over medium heat, or in a 350°F oven for 3 to 6 minutes, until they just begin to turn a light brown. Set them aside to cool.

An hour before baking, place a baking stone or baking steel on the middle oven rack if baking schiacciata (no stone needed for focaccia) and preheat 500°F. For schiacciata, dust a work surface with flour and, with floured hands, lift under one of the dough balls, cradling it, and transfer it to the floured work surface. Begin dimpling the dough from the center to the corners, dusting with additional flour as needed to prevent sticking. Rest for 60-second intervals, if needed, to allow the dough to relax. Dimple around the inner perimeter of the dough, leaving a ½-inch border undimpled. Use your fingertips to guide the dough into an oblong shape, coming to a point at each end, forming a canoe-shaped shell. Dust a baking peel or the back of smooth cutting board with flour, semolina, or cornmeal, and, with floured hands, gently lift and transfer the dough to the floured peel or cutting board.

Break or cut 4 ounces (113 grams) of Camembert (or Brie) into about 8 pieces and distribute them over the surface of the dough. Cover the cheese with 8 whole leaves of basil. Place 3 pear halves on top of the cheese and basil. Then divide 4 ounces (113 grams) of the blue cheese into 12 chunks and place 4 pieces around each of the pear halves. (If making the focaccia version, use all the pear halves, basil, and cheese).

Slide the schiacciata directly onto the baking stone and bake for 8 minutes. Rotate the dough for an even bake and continue baking for an additional 6 to 8 minutes, until the edge of the dough is golden brown and the underside of the crust is also golden brown (the focaccia will take longer, 20 to 25 minutes). While the schiacciata is baking, warm the maple syrup to about 100°F, or lukewarm. Transfer the baked schiacciata to a cutting board and evenly distribute the toasted pecan halves over the surface, but not on top of the pears. Drizzle about 2 tablespoons of maple syrup over the whole pie, especially over the pears. Cut it into 4 to 6 pieces and serve while topping and baking the second schiacciata.

Note: If making the focaccia variation, follow the method on page 151 for how to remove it from the pan and cut it into 12 squares.

Poaching the Pears

Juice of 1 ½ lemons
(3 tablespoons), divided

5 cups water

½ cup maple syrup

1 tablespoon granulated sugar

1 cinnamon stick, or ½ teaspoon
cinnamon

½ teaspoon vanilla extract

¼ teaspoon grated nutmeg

¼ teaspoon almond extract

Fill a small bowl with cold water and the juice of 1 lemon (or 2 tablespoons lemon juice). Cut off the stems and peel each Bosc pear by pulling a vegetable peeler from the neck down and then around the bottom in 1 or 2 smooth strokes. Then cut the pear in half lengthwise and core each half using a small melon baller or spoon. Place each half in the lemon water.

For the poaching liquid, fill a 2-quart pot with 5 cups of water and add the maple syrup, sugar, cinnamon, vanilla extract, nutmeg, almond extract, and remaining lemon juice. Bring to a simmer over medium-high heat. Use a slotted spoon to transfer the pears from the lemon water into the poaching liquid. Some pears may bob to the top, so either cut a piece of baking parchment into a round the same diameter as the pot and use it to seal in the heat, or just flip over the pears every 2 minutes.

Poach for 10 to 12 minutes and test the pears with a knife—they should be tender enough for the knife to slide in, but still be firm (because they'll be cooked again on the schiacciata). Use a slotted spoon to transfer each pear out of the poaching liquid and into an empty bowl (do not place the pears into cold water, or you'll wash off the flavor from the poaching liquid). Let the pears cool at room temperature for 5 minutes, then refrigerate until assembly.

Lee Hunzinger

Zoli Stromboli

Makes 2 large Stromboli

Stromboli was a villain in *Pinocchio,* and it's also the name of a volcanic island off the coast of Sicily and was even the name of a steamy Ingrid Bergman movie of the 1950s, but for most Americans, it's the name of a rolled-up, spiral pizza bread—a kind of pizza hoagie, if you will. Its origins arguably lie in Essington, a suburb of Philadelphia, at a place called Romano's Pizzeria and Italian Restaurant, though others have laid claim to its invention as well (of course—think how many people have claimed to be the inventor of the Reuben sandwich). In a sense, a Stromboli is a variant of the more well-known calzone, but more and more pizzerias are now making it, because not only is it delicious, but where could you get a better name for anything than "Stromboli"? Some of the best Stromboli in the country are found at the Dallas pizzeria Zoli's, where Lee Hunzinger serves as executive pizzaiolo for the PILF Restaurant Group, which owns both Zoli's and Cane Rosso, two of the great multi-location pizza restaurants in Texas.

Lee grew up in a restaurant family on Long Island and as a teenager discovered his passion specifically for all things pizza. Eventually he took his talents to Texas, where he also became one of the many members of the World Pizza Champions Team, and he continues to perfect his craft by omnivorously visiting and practicing with many of the other pizza giants in the industry. When I first met Lee at Pizza Expo, I was immediately impressed by his blend of humility and confidence in his abilities—he knows how good his work is, and many of his peers consider him a pizza genius, but his self-effacing manner and generous spirit are refreshing. While he has won many awards for his pizzas, I was alerted to his Stromboli by Apizza Scholls's Brian Spangler (see pages 51 and 146), who told me that Lee's version blew all others out of the water. We asked Lee to demonstrate his technique on *Pizza Talk*, which he did, so we now have a benchmark for a Stromboli that I'd happily present to Ingrid Bergman were she still with us (oh, how I wish . . .).

By the way, one of Lee's secrets is the sesame seeds on the crust. As we all know, sometimes it's the little things that make the difference.

Of course, this tribute version is only as good as the practice and effort that one puts into it, because so much of what makes this recipe work is the dough stretching and rolling technique that Lee makes look easy. It is, and it isn't, easy—but it is achievable and worth the effort, especially for those who love hoagies as much as I do. As a born-and-bred Philadelphian, I can attest to the importance of having a secret hoagie spread (page 44) in your repertoire, which is probably my main contribution to this tribute recipe and to this book. Have it on hand, because once you use it, you'll want to put it on many other pizzas and sandwiches. It certainly makes this Stromboli pop, and—dare I say it without over-promising—it might change your life.

New York Pizza Dough (page 30), made at least a day ahead

6 ounces (170 grams) Italian sausage links (sweet or spicy)

2 tablespoons olive oil

6 ounces (170 grams) deli ham or capicola, sliced thin

8 ounces (227 grams) whole milk mozzarella, shredded (about 4 cups)

4 ounces (113 grams) soppressata or other spicy salami, sliced thin

1 medium size sweet onion, julienned

24 fresh basil leaves

6 ounces (170 grams) Genoa salami, sliced thin

4 ounces (113 grams) pepperoni, sliced thin

4 Roma tomatoes, sliced thin

Hoagie Spread (page 44)

¼ cup sesame seeds

¼ cup chopped Italian parsley

Three hours before making the Stromboli, remove the pizza dough from the refrigerator and divide it into 2 (18-ounce, 510-gram) pieces. Mist a sheet pan with oil spray, then form the dough into tight dough balls and place them on the pan. Mist the dough balls with the oil spray and cover loosely with plastic wrap. Set the pan aside at room temperature to proof for about 3 hours.

While the dough is proofing, preheat the oven to 400°F and lay out the sausage links on a sheet pan or in a cast-iron skillet. Bake for 12 to 16 minutes, until they are firm and springy to the touch and turning golden brown on the outside. Remove the pan and set the links aside to cool. In the meantime, gather the remaining fillings.

An hour before baking the Stromboli, preheat the oven to 500°F. Rub the work surface with 1 teaspoon of olive oil to make a large oil slick, about 20 inches in diameter. Oil your hands, then place one of the dough balls on the surface and press it with your palms to flatten it. Use your fingertips to dimple the dough, from the center to all four corners, into a rectangle. You can also use the flat of your hands to press it out. If the dough shrinks back, let it rest for 2 to 3 minutes, then continue opening it wider until it forms a rectangle about 14 inches wide and 12 inches long. The dough should be thicker toward the bottom of the rectangle (closest to you)—about ⅓ inch thick, whereas the rest of the dough should be just under ¼ inch thick. Lightly brush the surface of the dough with olive oil.

Begin layering the filling ingredients over the lower third of the dough—the section closest to you (the thicker section)—with a single layer of sliced ham, leaving a border about 1 inch wide around the bottom and sides of the dough uncovered. Distribute a layer of mozzarella over the ham—just enough to lightly cover it. Add a layer of soppressata or spicy salami over the cheese, followed by another sprinkling of cheese. Distribute strips of the sweet onion and the 12 fresh basil leaves, as well as a layer of Genoa salami, followed by another sprinkle of cheese. Add a layer of pepperoni or any other sliced meat, as well as a layer of sliced tomatoes and a drizzle of hoagie spread, followed by another sprinkle of cheese.

Begin rolling up the Stromboli by pressing out and stretching the uncovered border of dough at the bottom and lifting it over the filling to cover it (don't worry if it tears—just patch it up and continue), pressing it into the border of uncovered dough around the filling. Gently place your fingers under the bottom of the filled section and, with a gentle pull to stretch the dough slightly, lift it up and over the folded section. Pinch the dough on both ends of the roll-up to seal it. Gently pull the folded section toward you to slightly stretch out the remaining dough and fold it over again, rolling it up. Continue stretching and rolling until the dough is fully rolled, with the seam side facing down on the work surface to seal it. Use a knife to trim off any unfilled dough on either side.

Cover a sheet pan with baking parchment or a silicone baking pad and carefully lift the Stromboli onto and along one side of the length of the pan, giving it a slight crescent-like curve. Repeat this process with the other piece of dough (or save it for later by returning it to the refrigerator). Prior to baking, brush the surface of the Strombolis with olive oil and generously sprinkle sesame seeds over the top. Use a serrated knife to cut three parallel diagonal slits across the top of the dough, cutting only as deep as the first layer of filling. Garnish with a sprinkling of chopped parsley and bake for 15 to 18 minutes, until the dough is golden brown and very firm and springy to the touch. Transfer the baked Stromboli to a cutting board and let it cool for at least 5 minutes before slicing it into 1 to 2-inch sections and serving.

Deconstructed Pizza alla Francis Mallmann

Serves 4 to 8

A regular contributor to the *Pizza Quest* website, Brad English is also one of our co-founders, along with Jeff Michael. He and Jeff have produced all the videos on our site as well as the *Pizza Talk* Zoom series. Brad's columns are our version of "If I can do it, so can you," in which he describes how, with no formal training outside of just being a hungry guy looking to make a good pizza, he comes up with all sorts of spur-of-the-moment ideas. When he got his small Forno Bravo wood-fired oven a few years ago, he became downright dangerous (in a good way), and his family benefited greatly from some of the amazing pizzas and other dishes he created in it. Here is an excerpt from his column called "A Francis Mallmann Moment," followed by my tribute version of his epiphany for everyone who does not own a WFO (yes, that's my fellow fire-freak's abbreviation for "wood-fired oven"):

There was a visual moment in an episode of the first season of Netflix's wonderful Chef's Table *about the brilliant, iconoclastic chef, Francis Mallmann. This moment is never spoken about in the narration, no dialogue, but it jumped off the screen and hit me like a ton of hot coals. I pressed pause and backed it up. "Did you see that?" I asked my wife. She didn't. She was actually playing Candy Crush while sitting there, supposedly watching the show with me.*

"There. Look!" Mallmann was cooking a dough right on the coals of a hot, open wood fire pit, at what looked like one of the most amazing spots on the planet Earth by a small open shack with a deck of sorts at a lake on an isolated Patagonian island that his family owns. Crazy! The camera shot floats over the lake, capturing this beautifully unique place as Francis and his assistants build a fire and begin cooking things, including bread dough, out there over and in this huge open fire. Clearly the man has this down to a system and an art. I have thrown a steak on the coals, sure, but a soft dough? This was a first, but where "Sir Francis" went, I had to follow.

"He just threw the dough on the coals and look, it puffed up—charred, but with a couple whacks of his knife it looks..." I stopped babbling, as one of the next shots in the montage showed him topping the dough with some greens, sliced red onions, and slices of what appeared to be burnt oranges and, then, dousing it all with a generous pour of olive oil. Let me just say the whole thing caused quite an epiphany in my mind! "HE JUST MADE A PIZZA! He made a pizza on an open wood fire on the ground next to a lake in the rain!!"

My wife was less impressed than I was but tried to give me some obligatory moral support, until I replayed it again—and then again. Apparently, if you are playing Candy Crush while pretending to watch a show, it can be annoying to have the show rewound more than once! I'm mostly exaggerating; she knows by now that I'm insane when it comes to food.

"I'll have to try that sometime," I told her.

So, I tried it. I had some leftover dough, and I decided to throw it on the coals in my wood-fired Primavera 60. Guess what? It worked. Thirty seconds or so on one side and then I flipped it over. Some coals stuck to it as it flipped. After another 30 or so seconds I pulled it out of the oven with some long tongs! A knock or two on the hearth to shake off the coals and there it was—a puffy dough with some nice char. "Cool!"

Perhaps I was lucky that I had this extra dough after earlier roasting some mixed seafood and Spanish chorizo in a cast-iron pan in the 800-degree WFO, because what was left over in the pan was some fabulous broth. I tore off a piece of the charred dough and used it to sop up the nectar. There were some little roasted bits of seafood in there also. So, the next bite was a torn piece of dough dipped in the broth and topped with a shrimp and a slice of the chorizo. The bite after that got a little drizzle of olive oil, a roasted mussel, a piece of chorizo, and a bit of basil. "Oh my God—this is a pizza!" I thought, intoxicated with the flavors. I then noticed my wife putting a little shard of fresh mozzarella on a torn piece of the dough and scraping up some tomato sauce from her plate. Aha, she was all in!

"This is a pizza! It's a fresh hot dough with stuff on it!" I blurted. She smiled.

If you are among the blessed WFO community (and even if you're not), you can see the whole article by going to our site (www.pizzaquest.com) and typing, "Francis Mallmann" in the search window, and following along. Till then, here's my tribute to Brad's pizza epiphany, made in a home oven.

Classic White Dough (page 26), made at least a day ahead

1 pound (16 ounces/ 454 grams) spicy sausage links

1 large or 2 small Fresno chili peppers or red jalapeños, seeded and cut into strips

1 large white or yellow onion, julienned

1 can or bottle of beer

8 ounces (227 grams) large, uncooked shrimp, shell on

1 pound (16 ounces /454 grams) fresh mussels or Manila or cherrystone clams

1 pound (16 ounces/454 grams) cleaned squid (calamari) or scallops

12 cloves garlic, divided (8 cloves sliced thin, 4 cloves pressed or minced)

1 teaspoon chili pepper flakes (optional)

1 teaspoon paprika

1 large lemon (preferably organic), seeded and quartered

½ cup chopped Italian parsley

1 large eggplant, cut into thin slices (about ¼ inch)

½ cup olive oil

¼ teaspoon ground black pepper

Crushed Tomato Pizza Sauce (page 42)

4 large tomatoes, heirloom if possible

8 ounces (227 grams) fresh mozzarella (fior di latte) or burrata cheese

24 fresh basil leaves

Three hours before baking, remove the dough from the refrigerator. Divide it into 9 (4-ounce/113-gram) pieces. Lightly mist a sheet pan with vegetable oil spray, then form the pieces into tight dough balls and place them on the sheet pan. Mist the dough balls with the oil spray and cover loosely with plastic wrap. Set aside to proof at room temperature for about 3 hours.

Preheat the oven to 550°F or as hot as it will allow. Cut the sausage links into 1½-inch pieces and place them in a cast-iron pan, ovenproof baking dish, or Dutch oven. Add the chili peppers and onion. Bake without a lid for 20 to 30 minutes, until the sausage is brown and crisp and the onions and peppers are soft. Add half the beer and cook for 5 additional minutes. Remove the pan from the oven and set it aside to cool.

Thoroughly wash all the shellfish and place them in another large cast-iron pan or ovenproof Dutch oven. Add the sliced garlic, chili flakes (if using), paprika, lemon quarters, remaining beer, and parsley (reserving a small amount for garnish). Bake as you did for the sausage (lid off) for 20 to 30 minutes, until the shellfish has opened, the shrimp has turned pink, and the juices are bubbling. Set the pan aside to cool. Taste the broth and add salt and pepper to taste.

Place the eggplant slices in a large bowl. Add ¼ cup olive oil, ½ teaspoon kosher salt, and ground black pepper, and toss to coat the pieces. Lay the pieces flat on 1 or 2 sheet pans and bake as soon as the seafood and sausage are done. Bake for about 8 minutes, then flip the pieces over with a pair of tongs and bake for an additional 6 to 10 minutes, until the eggplant softens and begins to char. Remove from the oven and use a metal spatula to transfer and stack the slices on a platter, domino-style. Set aside until service.

An hour before you plan to serve the pizza, place a baking stone or baking steel into the oven and preheat to 550°F or as hot as it will allow. While the oven is preheating, warm the tomato sauce over low heat. Slice the tomatoes and the fresh mozzarella (or burrata) into ¼-inch thick discs. Cover a platter with a layer of the sliced tomatoes. Sprinkle them with salt and pepper to taste, then add a layer of whole basil leaves, followed by a layer of the sliced cheese. Repeat this layering with the remaining tomatoes, basil, and cheese. Keep the platter refrigerated until service.

Just prior to baking the dough, reheat the sausage and seafood by covering them in their pans or Dutch ovens and heating on the stove over medium-low heat.

Whisk ¼ cup olive oil with the pressed or minced garlic and ¼ teaspoon salt. Dust the work surface with flour and, with floured hands, flatten all the dough balls to about ¾ inch thick. Brush the tops of the flattened pieces with the garlic oil, then press out the dough pieces with your fingertips to extend them to about 6 inches in diameter and ¼ to ⅓ inch thick. Bake as many as will fit on the baking stone for 4 to 6 minutes, until they puff and begin to char. Transfer them to a cutting board. Repeat the baking steps with the remaining pieces.

While the dough is baking, transfer the sauce, sausage, and seafood to serving bowls, along with the sliced tomatoes and the platter of baked eggplant, as well as the just-baked pizza dough. Garnish the platters with the chopped parsley. Bring out the hot crusts and serve. The guests can construct their "deconstructed" pizzas as they choose.

Epilogue

The Eleventh Commandment of *Pizza Quest*

It is more about the quest than it is about the pizza, and the quest never ends.

Acknowledgments

As always, this was a team effort, as evidenced by the more than 40 collaborators, creators, and photographers of these amazing "hero" pizzas, cited throughout. But, behind the scenes, I also want to thank the wonderful team at Andrews McMeel Universal, headed by publisher Kirsty Melville, who fully grokked the potential, uniqueness, and challenges of this book and chose to publish it despite those challenges. Senior editor, Allison Adler, provided superb guidance and perspective throughout, and the team of Holly Swayne, Meg Daniels, Carol Coe, and Sarah Nessel all contributed to crafting this into a beautiful book. Also, thanks to photographer and friend Peter Taylor who worked with me in the Johnson & Wales baking labs to create the various instructional shots used throughout the book.

Thanks to my co-founders and partners in PizzaQuest Productions, Brad English and Jeff Michael. They have produced and recorded all of our on-the-road videos and, more recently, our Zoom interviews and podcasts, as well as contributing many articles and much time to our website (in partnership with Forno Bravo Ovens), Pizzaquest.com. The three of us started *Pizza Quest* over twelve years ago but have been on our own personal pizza quests for most of our lives. This book is the latest manifestation of that collective journey.

Thanks also to the many pizza luminaries and thought leaders who appeared on Pizza Talk and Pizza Quest whose recipes did not appear in this collection, but whose work equally leavens the loaf and broadens my horizons. This group includes the editors of the two leading pizza trade journals, *Pizza Today* and *PMQ*, and all-around pizza maven, Scott Wiener, a frequent guest and contributor to *Pizza Quest*, and the most networked and knowledgeable guy I know in the pizza world. Enormous thanks, also, to Peter Lachapelle, Bill Oakley, and Jeremy White, the producers of the annual International Pizza Expo, where I first met many of the stars who appeared on our shows and in this book.

Also, thanks to my friends and colleagues at Johnson & Wales University in Charlotte, NC, who are all on their own quests, fueled by a similar creative passion for their various subjects. What a stimulating place to work for the past 25 years, and what inspiring people with whom to work.

Finally, as always, thanks to my wife, Susan, who shares my restless, relentless, never-ending search for the perfect pizza and, with her much finer-tuned palate, contributes mightily to the recipe testing (and tasting) in these pages.

Metric Conversions and Equivalents

Approximate Metric Equivalents

Volume

¼ teaspoon......................................1 milliliter
½ teaspoon............................... 2.5 milliliters
¾ teaspoon ....4 milliliters
1 teaspoon.....................................5 milliliters
1¼ teaspoons ....6 milliliters
1½ teaspoons ....7.5 milliliters
1¾ teaspoons............................. 8.5 milliliters
2 teaspoons................................. 10 milliliters
1 tablespoon (½ fluid ounce)...............15 milliliters
2 tablespoons (1 fluid ounce)..............30 milliliters
¼ cup ....60 milliliters
⅓ cup ....80 milliliters
½ cup (4 fluid ounces).....................120 milliliters
⅔ cup...160 milliliters
¾ cup...180 milliliters
1 cup (8 fluid ounces)..................... 240 milliliters
1¼ cups......................................300 milliliters
1½ cups (12 fluid ounces) ....360 milliliters
1⅔ cups ....400 milliliters
2 cups (1 pint) .... 460 milliliters
3 cups...................................... 700 milliliters
4 cups (1 quart)..................................95 liter
1 quart plus ¼ cup ....1 liter
4 quarts (1 gallon) ....3.8 liters

Weight

¼ ounce ....7 grams
½ ounce ....14 grams
¾ ounce...21 grams
1 ounce ....28 grams
1¼ ounces..35 grams
1½ ounces ....42.5 grams
1⅔ ounces ....45 grams
2 ounces .... 57 grams
3 ounces ....85 grams
4 ounces (¼ pound)...........................113 grams
5 ounces ....142 grams
6 ounces ....170 grams
7 ounces ....198 grams
8 ounces (½ pound)...........................227 grams
16 ounces (1 pound)......................... 454 grams
35.25 ounces (2.2 pounds)....................1 kilogram

Length

⅛ inch...3 millimeters
¼ inch...6 millimeters
½ inch ....1¼ centimeters
1 inch...2½ centimeters
2 inches.......................................5 centimeters
2½ inches......................................6 centimeters
4 inches.......................................10 centimeters
5 inches.......................................13 centimeters
6 inches.......................................15¼ centimeters
12 inches (1 foot) .... 30 centimeters

Metric Conversion Formulas

To Convert	Multiply
Ounces to grams	Ounces by 28.35
Pounds to kilograms	Pounds by .454
Teaspoons to milliliters	Teaspoons by 4.93
Tablespoons to milliliters	Tablespoons by 14.79
Fluid ounces to milliliters	Fluid ounces by 29.57
Cups to milliliters	Cups by 236.59
Cups to liters	Cups by .236
Pints to liters	Pints by .473
Quarts to liters	Quarts by .946
Gallons to liters	Gallons by 3.785
Inches to centimeters	Inches by 2.54

Oven Temperatures

To convert Fahrenheit to Celsius, subtract 32 from Fahrenheit, multiply the result by 5, then divide by 9.

Description	Fahrenheit	Celsius	British Gas Mark
Very cool	200°	95°	0
Very cool	225°	110°	¼
Very cool	250°	120°	½
Cool	275°	135°	1
Cool	300°	150°	2
Warm	325°	165°	3
Moderate	350°	175°	4
Moderately hot	375°	190°	5
Fairly hot	400°	200°	6
Hot	425°	220°	7
Very hot	450°	230°	8
Very hot	475°	245°	9

Common Ingredients and Their Approximate Equivalents

1 cup uncooked white rice = 185 grams
1 cup all-purpose flour = 125 grams
1 stick butter (4 ounces • ½ cup • 8 tablespoons) = 115 grams
1 cup butter (8 ounces • 2 sticks • 16 tablespoons) = 225 grams
1 cup brown sugar, firmly packed = 220 grams
1 cup granulated sugar = 200 grams

Information compiled from a variety of sources, including *Recipes into Type* by Joan Whitman and Dolores Simon (Newton, MA: Biscuit Books, 1993); *The New Food Lover's Companion* by Sharon Tyler Herbst (Hauppauge, NY: Barron's, 2013); and *Rosemary Brown's Big Kitchen Instruction Book* (Kansas City, MO: Andrews McMeel, 1998).

Index